Zebra Finches

Cyril Rogers

John Bartholomew and Son Limited
Edinburgh

© John Bartholomew & Son Ltd.
First published in Great Britain 1977 by
John Bartholomew and Son Ltd., 12 Duncan Street,
Edinburgh, EH9 1TA
Reprinted 1981, 1982, 1984

ISBN 0 7028 1085 1

Printed in Great Britain by John Bartholomew & Son Limited

Contents

Chapter 1

The Zebra Finch
in its Native Home

Latin: *Taeniopygia guttata castanotis*

English: Zebra Finch sometimes called Chestnut-eared Finch

French: Diamant mandarin

Dutch: Zebravink

Belguim: Moineau mandarin and Diamant mandarin

German, Danish and Swedish: Zebrafink

Colour description
Cock Beak: coral red. Top of head: grey with each feather edged
with dark grey. Back of neck: grey. Large ear patches rich chestnut
brown with a black line running from eyes down one side, this black
line is followed by a wider white stripe and the beak side is edged
with a further thin black line. Throat and upper chest: finely barred
with black and white terminating with a black bar about one eighth
of an inch (3·2 mm) wide right across the chest from flank to flank.
Lower chest and abdomen: white tinged with fawn at thighs, vent
and under tail coverts. Flanks: deep chestnut heavily spotted with
white round dots. Back: grey with a brownish tinting, flights and
secondaries dark grey, rump white merging to black and white at
sides. Central tail feathers white widely barred with black, outer
tail feathers blackish grey. Iris: red brown. Feet and legs: dark
orange red. Length about 4¼″–4½″ (10·7–11·3 cm).
Hen Beak: orange red. General colouring same as cock except chestnut ear patches are absent and the breast and flanks are pale grey
instead of the striping and flank markings.

The young are duller editions of the hen without the eye stripes and the beak is black which changes to red when they assume their full adult plumage at eight to twelve weeks old.

Sub species There are a number of sub species but it is difficult to place the exact number of clearly recognisable forms. Some ornithologists give two sub species whereas others such as Neville W. Cayley, Serventy and Whitall, give ten or more. However all writers agree on a sub species from the Island of Timor. The Timor Zebra Finch *T. g. guttata* which is coloured distinctly from *T. g. castanotis*. The cock has silvery grey on the throat and upper breast, the sides of the neck having only faint black stripes and there are a few fine lines on the upper breast but no chest bar. The grey colouring on the back is somewhat darker and has a heavy brownish tinting. The hen is similar to the other species although the overall colouring is more brown in tone. Other sub species are said to have slight differences in colour shades and distribution and vary somewhat in size, but are not so distinct in colour as *T. g. guttata*. Several different mutant colour forms have been recorded amongst wild flocks in Australia.

Distribution Zebra Finches are to be found over a very wide area of the Australian Continent including Flores, Sumba and South West Islands, and the Island of Timor. It seems that they are not found in parts of the South East and South West coastal areas or in North East Queensland. Zebra Finches have a wider distribution than any of the other Australian Finches and are the commonest species of bird.

They prefer to live in open grassland where there are some trees and bushes together with access to rivers, ponds or water holes. They also live near small settlements, farms, cattle compounds and anywhere where water is available to them. Their food consists of the seeds of many grasses and weeds found growing in both cultivated and uncultivated areas. Whilst searching for seeds they find and eat numerous small insects, caterpillars and grubs, and these are eaten in much larger quantities during the breeding periods. Zebra Finches drink and bathe very frequently and a constant water supply is essential for them all through the year in whatever area they live.

Although they nest in a variety of places such as hollows in trees, holes in buildings, and in the bulky nests of large birds, they have a preference to make their nests in thick or spiney bushes. Being sociable birds their nests may be found in small colonies of up to a dozen nests in a single large thorn bush. The nest itself is a small untidy

8

Cock

Hen

The difference between cock and hen birds

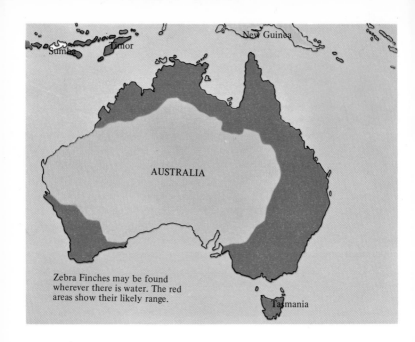

AUSTRALIA

Zebra Finches may be found
wherever there is water. The red
areas show their likely range.

dome structure with an entrance tunnel and made of stiff grasses
lines with vegetable down, wool, feathers or soft grasses. If these
materials are not available in their actual nesting area they will use
any suitable things that are on hand. Three to seven eggs are laid
and are incubated for about twelve days both parents sharing this
duty and also that of feeding the chicks. Young birds fly from the
nest when about three weeks old and then they are fed mainly by
the cock until they can feed for themselves. During this period the
hen will produce another clutch of eggs which she incubates mainly
on her own until the cock is free from the responsibility of feeding
the first brood.

Zebra Finches always like to roost under shelter and during their
non breeding seasons they will either use their old breeding nests,
make rough new ones, or use deserted, nests of other species as
sleeping places. This particular roosting behaviour is characteristic
of many small species of Finch-like and similar birds found in many
countries. It would seem that by using roosting nests Zebra Finches
obtain considerable protection from night predators.

Chapter 2

Some Historical Notes

At what date the first wild type Grey Zebra Finches were imported into Great Britain and Europe, or who was first to breed from them, is a matter of conjecture. As far back as 1805 the French Naturalist, L. J. P. Vieillot described Zebra Finches, although he gave them a different name 'Le Bengali mouchete' but it is not known whether his description was taken from live birds or from skins. They were also described by John Gould in one of his papers in 1838 some two years before he brought his first Budgerigars to Great Britain. In my opinion they were originally imported commercially between 1840–1850 as during this period the many and varied species of Australian flora and fauna were coming into Europe in considerable quantities. Within a decade or two of these dates Zebra Finches were breeding freely in aviaries in both Great Britain and Europe. The late Allen Silver (1878–1969) who was one of our leading authorities on Foreign birds told me that 'Foreign Cage Birds' by C. W. Gedney published in 1879 contained the first full account of Zebra Finches in the English language. This supports the fact that Zebra Finches were free aviary breeders in the years between 1850 and 1880. In addition to being very good parents to their own young they would also rear unquestionably the young of other more rare seeding species. Because of this extremely useful trait the majority of breeders of small Foreign birds of that time always kept a few pairs of Zebra Finches to act as foster parents. Consequently Zebra Finches were widely known and good numbers were bred each year so that stocks of aviary bred birds were always available in the Fancy at very reasonable prices. Some colour mutations had occurred towards the end of the nineteenth century but according to Dr. Russ they were of little importance although he did not qualify his statement.

During the first half of this century the keeping and breeding of Zebra Finches steadily increased aided undoubtedly by the appearance of a number of interesting colour mutations which I shall be discussing fully in later chapters. Aviary bred stocks were strengthened from time to time by the addition of birds imported from various parts of Australia and these importations undoubtedly contained examples of many of the sub species.

In 1952 the cult of Zebra Finches had become so widespread in

Great Britain that a band of devoted breeders met and formed The Zebra Finch Society for the development and improvement of these birds in captivity. Its first President was the late Allen Silver who held the Office until his death, and the first Secretary was the late Stan Moulson with F. G. Cannon as Treasurer and A. J. Wilkins as Chairman. The formation of this Specialist Society was a milestone in the progress of Zebra Finches and from its inception their popularity both as aviary and exhibition birds increased beyond all expectations. The Society organised the exhibition side by formulating show rules, exhibition standards, colour standards, closed coded coloured metal rings, show cages and by giving patronage to local and other show promoting societies. Its Year Book and other publications gave much practical information on the breeding methods for producing Zebra Finches in cages and aviaries and the various colour mutations. Stemming from the initial work of the Zebra Finch Society came numerous Area bodies all of which are affiliated to the Parent Society.

The next important step on the road to success for Zebra Finches was the declaration by the Zebra Finch Society in 1958 that these birds should no longer be classed as Foreign birds but as a fully domesticated species. This declaration was in due course accepted species. This declaration was in due course accepted by all other countries where Zebra Finches were being bred. At one time only the odd few pairs of Zebra Finches were to be seen at Cage Bird Shows and then in mixed classes with other small Foreign birds. At the present time most shows have a separate section for Zebra Finches with eight to over twenty classes and some of the larger shows actually have two or three hundred or more pairs on show. The most outstanding achievement in the exhibition world was when in 1972 a pair of White Zebra Finches bred by the exhibitor, L. Harris of Birmingham, gained the Supreme Award at the National Exhibition of Cage and Aviary Birds, Alexandra Palace, London. This fine win did much to boost the image of Zebra Finches as first class exhibition and breeding birds. In 1974 The Zebra Finch Society staged its own first all Zebra Finch Club Show and this proved to be a most successful event.

Undoubtedly the Zebra Finch Society has had much influence in making Zebra Finches popular birds with overseas bird breeders and Specialist Societies for Zebra Finches have been established in Australia, America, Holland, Belgium, Germany, Sweden and doubtlessly other countries will soon be following. The exchange of ideas world wide always has a beneficial effect on any species and

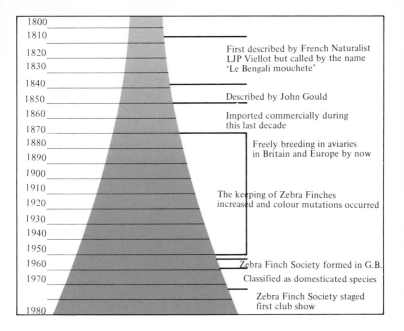

1800	
1810	
1820	First described by French Naturalist LJP Viellot but called by the name 'Le Bengali mouchete'
1830	
1840	
1850	Described by John Gould
1860	Imported commercially during this last decade
1870	
1880	Freely breeding in aviaries in Britain and Europe by now
1890	
1900	
1910	The keeping of Zebra Finches increased and colour mutations occurred
1920	
1930	
1940	
1950	
1960	Zebra Finch Society formed in G.B.
1970	Classified as domesticated species
1980	Zebra Finch Society staged first club show

Zebra Finches have gained substantially from this co-operation. A great deal of valuable data on Zebra Finches has been given to the Zebra Finch Fancy in articles and papers by Dr. K. Immelman of Switzerland and C. af Enehjelm of Denmark in both European and British publications. In America Prof. Val Clear is a leading authority on Zebra Finches and his writings have helped very considerably to popularise them in that country. Already several new mutations have been established in Europe by keen breeders and in due course it is hoped that these new coloured birds will also be bred in Great Britain and in time appear on our show benches.

In view of the above notes on the activities of The Zebra Finch Society I would strongly advise all breeders who are interested in the welfare of these delightful little domesticated birds to join The Zebra Finch Society.*

*See Appendix

13

Chapter 3

Breeding in captivity

I think it can safely be said that Zebra Finches as a whole are the most free breeders of all the domesticated species of cage and aviary birds. Nevertheless owing to the environmental changes they have undergone over the last few decades they do now need more care and thought than their wild caught ancestors seemed to have required.

Irrespective of any other factors the all important one is the physical fitness of the birds intended for breeding purposes. Like all livestock Zebra Finches are individual in their personal behaviour and development. This means that the breeding stock need not all come into breeding condition at precisely the same time no matter how much their owners may desire this to come about. Owners can of course do much to help their birds to gain peak condition by correct feeding and good general management. Here again foods and feeding will be discussed fully later.

It should be carefully noted that there is quite a difference between birds being in what is known as show condition and those in breeding condition. With the former state it is imperative that all the feathers are present and that they are clean, not faded, broken or missing, and that the toes and nails are all intact. Exhibition birds may also carry a little extra weight due to being confined to cages during the show season. Such birds are not necessarily in breeding condition although they look good to the eye. Birds in full breeding condition can of course also be perfect in feather although generally speaking their plumage is inclined to get a little ruffled even though the sexes may be housed apart. Physical signs of fitness with cock birds are bright eyes, activity, squabbling and continually making their funny little singing noises and calling to the hens. Hen birds are equally bright eyed, restless, quarrelsome, continually looking for nesting sites, carrying in their beaks any pieces of material that could be used for nest building including feathers from their companions which they are not adverse to pulling out. Any cocks and hens that are seen to be sitting or hopping about in a listless manner and taking little interest in their companions are cer-

Filling in a register is an important
part of bird breeding

tainly not ready for the arduous task of breeding.

When Zebra Finches have been housed in cages and particularly those which have been exhibited they should have a few weeks in a large flight or aviary before being used to breed. This period of freedom will help to remove surplus fat and get them in a good hard condition and it certainly helps to prevent egg binding in the hens. They will often attempt to reproduce and may even do so soon after they have assumed their full adult plumage although it is not wise to actually breed from them until they are nine to twelve months old. At this age the birds are fully mature and well able to produce fit healthy young of good quality. I often think that breeding failures can be traced to the use over a period of young birds that are not fully matured. It is imperative that all breeders should keep and maintain a stock breeding register if they are going to ensure the continued production of high class stock. This register need only be a simple one giving the colour, breeder, ring number and any other information on all the breeding birds. Each mated pair should be entered on a separate page with the dates of pairing, first egg, number of eggs and first chick hatched. The number of chicks raised with their ring numbers, any clear, addled or dead-in-shell eggs, can be recorded later, together with any details the breeder feels

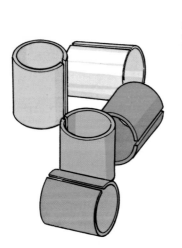

Split metal and
plastic rings

Closed metal
ring year-dated
and numbered

Closed colour-coded metal ring
year-dated and numbered
supplied to members from the
Zebra Finch Society

should be included. If any birds are sold, the name and address of the buyer can be usefully kept in the register. After a few seasons a complete picture of the stock's history will always be available to the breeder and will be of tremendous value when mating pairs for breeding. Close inbreeding can be avoided by reference to the register and any birds with noted undesirable features can be left out of future breeding programmes.

Whilst on the subject of records I think this is the time to write about rings and ringing. It will be realised that ringing young Zebra Finches with closed metal rings is the only sure way of positive identification. Both celluloid (plastic) and metal split rings are very good and serve a useful purpose but unfortunately they can come off. Should the breeder have difficulty for some reason or other in putting on closed metal rings then the split ones can be used. A careful watch should always be kept on the birds in case any rings come adrift, if they do they should be replaced immediately. In practice it is reasonably simple to slip on closed metal rings if the following method is carried out. After some trial and error the breeder will find the best age for putting the rings on their birds. I find the best time is when the chicks are just starting to feather with their flight feathers clearly showing. Chicks at this stage of develop-

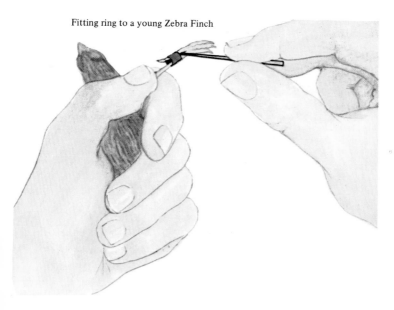

Fitting ring to a young Zebra Finch

ment are much easier to hold and their feet and legs are stronger but still very pliable. The chick to be ringed should be held firmly but gently in the palm of the hand taking one leg between the first finger and thumb. The ring is then slipped over the three longer front toes, along the leg and short hind toe which is then carefully pulled free from the ring with the aid of a sharpened matchstick or something similar. Mostly the chicks will accept this handling placidly but of course some may struggle and squeak a little. This squeaking is not caused by them being hurt but from resentment of being handled. When closed ringing is first tried the breeder may be a little apprehensive about the procedure but after a few rings have been slipped on it then becomes quite a simple job.

Many thousands of young Zebra Finches are ringed each year with closed coded metal rings which can be obtained through The Zebra Finch Society. These rings have a different colour each year and carry the breeder's own personal Zebra Finch Society code number together with the year, date and a number. For example, my code number is R.20 so for 1976 my rings are purple, the colour for that year, each stamped R.20 and Z.6.S. and numbered from 1 onwards. Because of the limited space on these small rings the year is incorporated in the Society's mark the figure 6 between the Z. and S. indicates 1976, and this is supported by the actual colour of the rings.

When the birds are flying in cage, pen or aviary the year of their breeding can easily be told by the colour of the rings. Sometimes more precise information is needed and this can be indicated by the use of split coloured celluloid (plastic) rings. These rings can be had in a wide range of colours and combinations of two or more colours. They are easy to put on birds of all ages and this is done with the aid of a small tool supplied with the rings by the Manufacturers. The young from each pair can be ringed with the same coloured split ring so the breeder will know by reference to the breeding register the parentage of any young birds in the flock without the trouble of catching them up and checking their ring numbers.

It is essential that the initial stock of birds are strong fit and vigorous and of reasonable quality and wherever possible closed ringed young birds of the previous season. At first the intending breeder may not be sure just what colour or colours to take up but this is of little importance as such a point can be decided at a later date. The great thing is to get practical experience with the general management and breeding of Zebra Finches in either cages, pens or aviaries. When the breeder has become experienced with keeping them then the colour or colours for the strain can be decided upon.

Because of the problem of birdroom space often experienced by Zebra Finch enthusiasts living in towns and cities, breeding in cages has become very widespread and popular. Undoubtedly cages offer the simplest and surest method of complete breeding control which is so essential for the production of colours and exhibition stock. In an aviary containing a number of pairs, twice as many nest boxes as there are pairs should be supplied, this gives the birds a choice and helps to prevent too much squabbling for nest sites. Unused boxes can be removed later when the birds have made their choice and used as replacements when needed.

If you have only a single pair of birds per cage only one nest box will be needed and this should be sited for easy access for general inspection and for ringing. There are several types of nest boxes available in bird stores or the handy person can make them quite easily. The usual type of nest box is a 5″ (13 cm) wooden cube with an entrance at the front and a hinged lid for inspection on the top. Some breeders like to have a round entrance hole about 1″ (2·5 cm) diameter with a short perch underneath whereas others like a half open front with or without a perch. Another design has half the front sloping backwards with an entrance hole in the centre and no perch. Plywood together with pine or deal boards are suitable for

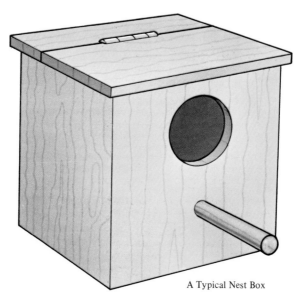

A Typical Nest Box

making nest boxes. These nest boxes are suitable for Zebra Finches breeding in all kinds of accommodation. In a planted aviary flight Zebra Finch pairs will often build their own natural nests, but these nests prevent inspection by the owner. The same applies to basket-work nests, which although used quite extensively at one period are now seldom seen. At various times Zebra Finches have been recorded to have nested in such things as Canary nest pans, Budgerigar nest boxes, coconut husks, plant pots, old tins, piles of hay, seed vessels and in fact anywhere that they can put nesting material.

Zebra Finches will use many kinds of small movable objects for nesting material such as dried grasses, straw, feathers, mosses, green food, twigs, string, wood splinters and shavings, pieces of dried droppings and even small stones. Some of these items are quite un-suitable and wherever possible should be kept out of reach of the breeding pairs. The best nesting materials are undoubtedly soft fried grasses, hay, mosses and small soft feathers, all of which are quite easy to obtain. Before each breeding season I always collect a few plastic bags full of clean dry and drying grasses from the local hedge-rows so I have a good supply on hand when needed. Before I put in the nest boxes I half fill them with the dried grasses and then supply the birds with a further quantity so they can complete their nest building. For lining I provide them with some small feathers and soft moss when I think they have done the initial building and this varies from two to seven days. Immediately the first eggs appear I remove all unused building material, this of course is quite easy in cages but more difficult in aviaries. The reason for this is to try and prevent the birds, mostly the cocks, from making sandwich nests and spoiling the clutches of eggs. This building of sandwich nests appears more likely to happen in cages than in aviaries as in the latter the birds have more to occupy their time and have space to fly.

The number of eggs laid per clutch will vary from three to eight or even more and the very large clutches are usually two clutches laid one directly after the other. Zebra Finch eggs are white in colour and oval in shape with one end slightly larger than the other. Both members of a pair share the duties of incubating and the feed-ing of the young. Incubation mostly starts after the laying of the second or third egg and is of some eleven to twelve days duration. There may be a few days difference between the hatching of the first and last chicks of a clutch according to the number of eggs and when incubation actually started.

When first hatched, young Zebra Finches are sparsely covered with down that varies from grey to white in colour, according to the

Zebra Finches will nest almost anywhere that they can build a nest. The items shown are what they usually choose.

variety. Young Zebra Finches develop very quickly and are usually ready to leave their nest box when between sixteen to eighteen days old; more quickly in the warm weather. Both parents will continue to feed their young for about a week until the hen lays again at which time the cock takes over until they can fend for themselves. Once in their breeding cycle Zebra Finch hens are prodigious producers of clutches of eggs but if strong vigorous young are required the adults should be stopped after having reared two full nests of chicks in a season. If the first two nests have only contained one or two young-sters then a third round is quite permissible and is usually most successful. It is not actually the laying of eggs that weakens the adult hen birds, but the feeding of full nests of growing chicks. Over breeding always has an adverse effect on the stamina of the adult birds and any young they produce are mostly of poor quality.

When they first come out of their nest boxes the young birds are not very strong and their sense of direction is rather poor and this can be a problem. Each year numerous young freshly flown Zebra Finches, together with other similar sized small birds, are drowned in water vessels during their first day or so out from the nest. If the drinking pots are too deep and a young bird happens in its clumsy flight to fall into a water pot its feather quickly become waterlogged and the bird drowns. This possibility indicates that all water containing vessels must be shallow, holding not more than about three quarters of an inch (1·75 cm) of water. There is also another danger that claims victims each year when breeding is carried out in flighted aviaries and particularly so if they are well planted. It is not unusual during the breeding season in this country to get sudden very heavy showers of rain. If a shower should occur when newly flown young are in a flight it is quite possible for them to drown, or die from becoming wet and chilled. The feathers of young Zebra Finches are soft and very absorbent and in rain quickly become soaked thereby preventing the birds from flying and forcing them down on to the wet flight floor. If possible, when wet showery weather is expected, young Zebra Finches should be confined to their sleeping quarters until you are quite sure they have their full power of flight.

A few days after nests of young birds are seen to be feeding satisfactorily on their own they should be removed from the care of their parents so that the adult birds can proceed unhampered with their next brood. If this is not done the chicks are most likely to worry their parents causing them to attack the youngsters in an effort to drive them away. Whilst this squabbling is going on the current nests of eggs may be neglected and very possibly spoiled. A further point to be remembered is that young birds if left in a breeding aviary may well attempt to nest long before they are really ready for the task of parenthood. As soon as the sex of the young birds can be definitely established they should be split up and housed in separate flights or aviaries until they are required for breeding. This is quite easy with most colours as the markings on young cock birds soon start to be visible except of course with Whites and Albinos. By following this procedure the breeder will give the stock the greatest opportunity of developing to their fullest capacity. Segregated birds invariably go to nest much easier and settle down with their selected partners without trouble.

Chapter 4

The Dominant Colour Mutations

In addition to the Normal Grey which is Dominant over all colours there are two other Dominant characters—the Dominant Dilute (Silver and Cream) and the Crested. I will deal first of all with the Dilute character which alters the depth of colour in other mutations and then the Crest which is a feather change, again applicable to all colours. The Dominant Dilute character is said to have been first noticed in the Normal Grey form giving a silvery grey shade and I will discuss these first.

Dominant Silver (Dilute Normal Grey)
Colour description
Cock Beak: coral red. Top of head: silver grey with each feather edged with darker silver grey. Back of neck: silver grey. Large ear patches light orange to pale cream with a blackish line running from the eyes down one side, this blackish line is followed by a wider white stripe and the beak side is edged with a further thin blackish line. Throat and upper chest: finely barred with blackish grey and white terminating with a blackish grey bar about one eighth of an inch (3 mm) wide right across the chest from flank to flank. Lower chest, abdomen and undertail coverts: white. Flanks: chestnut, heavily spotted with round white dots. Back: silver grey, flights and secondaries silver grey, rump: white merging to black and white at sides. Central tail feathers, white, widely barred with dark silver, outer tail feathers darker silver. Iris: red-brown to brown. Feet and legs: pale orange, may vary in depth.

Hen Beak: orange red. General colouring same as the cock except the colour of the ear patches is absent and the breast and flanks are pale silver grey instead of striping and flank markings.

The Dominant Silver was first noted as a mutation in Australia, although the exact place or date have not as far as I can ascertain been recorded. Undoubtedly examples of the Dominant Silver were imported into Europe where they soon multiplied and eventually arrived in Great Britain. During this development period a further Dilute mutation occurred in Europe, this time a Recessive one, all of which helped to confuse the origin of the Dominant Silver. There has been some speculation as to whether the Silver form of the Dominant Dilute actually appeared first. There is a possibility that the Cream form was the original and that the Silver naturally came from them. In the absence of precise details this is a matter of pure speculation. In Europe this colour form is known as Silber, Zilver and Argente, according to country.

The Dominant Dilute character which causes this particular colour phase operates in the usual manner of dominance and can be carried in either a single or double quantity. Both of these forms show the same visual colour, and it is only in their breeding where they differ. When a Silver with a single character for Silver is paired to a Normal Grey, half of their young are single character Silvers and the other half Normal Greys. The Normal Grey young from these pairings are just the same genetically as birds bred from two Normal Greys, in other words they do not carry any Silver character. Two single character Silvers paired together produce the theoretical expectation of 25% Double character Silver, 50% Single character Silver and 25% Normal Grey. A Double character Silver paired to a Normal Grey gives all single character Silver young. From this it will be seen that whenever a Silver is paired to any colour a percentage of their young must show the silver colouring.

When Dominant Silvers were first being bred in Great Britain the majority of them were of a good even true silver colour throughout and some extremely good birds were seen at the various shows. Over the past few years Silvers have steadily lost their popularity with breeders and exhibitors and consequently they are now only seen on infrequent occasions. Their loss of favour, is I feel sure, due to two factors with the most important being the difficulty now experienced in producing birds of good even colour. The second is the rise in popularity of the Dilute Fawn (Cream) which has been found far easier to breed with a good colour. As soon as it was discovered that Silvers paired to Fawn would produce in due course of time the delightful softly coloured Creams a large number of the best coloured Silvers were used for this purpose. This meant that fewer Silvers were bred and of them a large percentage showed a two tone colouring on mantle and wings no doubt due to the cross pairing. Such birds show distinct deep cream shadings on their upper parts and in fact are very difficult in certain lights to identify.

When a series of planned matings using only first class well coloured Normal Greys as mates for Silvers is made it should be possible once again to produce the desired level pure colour Silver.

Dominant Silver

25

The Silvers used for such pairings should be selected birds showing the best possible silver colour with few breaks in the shading. By using such birds it enhances the chance of the colour being passed on to their young helped by the fact that their mates are good Normal Greys. It does not matter which member of a pair is the Silver as with a Dominant character the sex of a bird has no influence on the transmission of that character. This fact is most helpful when building up a stud of exhibition Silvers.

In the initial stages of developing a stud I would suggest that a breeder commences with not less than four actual Silver birds for which Normal Grey mates will be required and these birds should be pure bred if possible. Much of the breaking of the shading in most varieties is due to continual outcrossing, the use of birds carrying other colour characters and not selecting the breeding stock for colour. The first season's breeding would produce Normal Greys and single character Silvers in approximately equal numbers. From these young the best coloured Silvers should be chosen for the following season's matings. Their Normal Grey nest mates should be very carefully examined for colour purity and only those which pass a stringent test in this respect should be retained. To make up the necessary pairs further pure Normal Greys should be obtained and this method should be carried out each breeding season. After a few years of this kind of carefully selected matings it is usually possible to begin the Silver to Silver pairings without loss of colour or type. As indicated at the commencement of this Chapter such pairings give 75% Silvers and 25% Normal Greys with some of the Silvers being double character birds. In the end the stud will be giving mainly Silvers and the need to outcross will only arise when some special feature is needed to be introduced.

Dominant Cream (Dilute Fawn)
Colour description
Cock Beak: coral red. Top of head: deep cream with each feather edged with darker cream. Back of neck: cream. Large ear patches, light orange to cream with a blackish line running from the eyes down one side, this blackish line is followed by a wider white stripe and the beak side is edged with a further thin blackish line. Throat and upper chest: finely barred with brownish-grey and white terminating with a brownish-grey bar about one eighth of an inch (3 mm) wide right across the chest from flank to flank. Lower chest and abdomen and under tail coverts: white. Flanks: chestnut, spotted heavily with round white dots. Back: cream, flights and secondaries

Dominant Cream

27

cream of a slightly deeper shade, rump white merging to brownish-black and white at sides. Central tail feathers white widely barred with dark cream, outer tail feathers darker cream. Iris: red-brown to brown. Feet and legs: pale orange, may vary in depth.

Hen Beak: orange red. General colouring same as the cock except the colour of the ear patches is absent and the breast and flanks are cream instead of striping and flank markings.

The Dominant Cream (Dilute Fawn) appears to be the result of combining the Dominant Dilute character with the Fawn. It is known that Creams can be bred by crossing Silvers with Fawns although in the first instance it could have been that the Silvers were derived from the Creams. I have not been able to discover any precise details of the origin of the Dominant Dilute character except that the mutation occurred in Australia. If particulars are not kept or published in the Fancy literature it is not possible to track down just where or how any new mutation came into being. At first the Creams did not seem to be very popular with exhibitors and it was the Silvers that were mostly seen on the show benches. However with the deterioration of the colour in Silvers the Creams started to forge ahead and at the present time they are much sought after both as aviary and exhibition birds.

In their actual production the Creams differ from Silvers as the Fawn character from which they are derived is Sex-linked as will be seen in the following Chapter. There can be both single and double character Creams with both genetical kinds having the same visual colouring. As a guide to the breeder I will describe how Cream strains can be created through obtaining the Dominant Dilute character via the Silver. By mating a single character Silver cock to a Fawn hen Normal Grey/Fawn and single character Silver/Cream cocks and Normal Grey and Fawn hens will result. The reverse pairing owing to the sex-linkage of the Fawn character gives quite a different expectation. A single character Silver hen paired to a Fawn cock gives Normal Grey/Fawn and single character Silver/Cream cocks and single character Cream and Fawn hens. To get Cream cocks a Fawn cock should be paired to a Cream hen and half their young will be Cream single character cocks and hens. It will be seen that as soon as Cream hens have been bred Creams of both sexes can be produced at will.

With the breeding of exhibition Creams the selection of the parent stock is most important not only for type but also for purity of overall colour. The Fawns used should be of a level medium fawn shade, neither too dark or too light and the Creams used should again be of a medium level colour with their markings clearly distinct. By making such a selection of breeding pairs a percentage of the young they produce should be of the desired medium cream and fawn shades. As with all mutations there are invariably some differences in the depth of the colours individual pairs produce in their young depending on the ancestry of the parent birds. I have found that amongst Fawns there is a strong tendency for their colour to fade if the birds are housed where they have access to strong sunlight. Although Creams are derived from Fawn stock they do not seem to suffer to any extent from this plumage fading so I can only come to the conclusion that this must be due to the Dominant Dilute character compound in their colour makeup. The soft colour shown by the Dominant Creams makes them most attractive for aviary or exhibition birds. If Cream strains are kept free from the mixture of other colours except of course Fawn the ultimate consistency of the colour of the birds will be very good. When matching pairs of Creams for exhibition purposes it is essential that both cock and hen show the same depth of cream colour.

The Crested

There can be a Crested form of the Normal Grey and all its colour mutations therefore the descriptions of the colours given in this and other Chapters are the same for the Crests. The information about Zebra Finches having small irregular tufts of feathers on their head was first given to me some years ago by that internationally famous ornithologist and bird artist Herman Heinzel who at the time was living in Andorra. Whilst in Spain he saw two Normal Grey cocks that had small rough crests on their heads. No details of their parentage were available but obviously they had been bred from other Crested birds. During the past few years Crested strains of Zebra Finches have been raised in several European countries and the mutation is now well established.

From information received from several sources it seems that the actual formation of the crest can vary from small tufts of raised feathers to the full circular crest. There is a similar variation to be found amongst the Crested Bengalese. I have in my possession a Normal Grey cock that has a full although small circular crest and this bird was bred by Herman Heinzel from a hen that has a large full crest like a Gloster Fancy Canary. Most of the Crests seem to be Normal Greys but I am sure it will not be very long before they will be appearing in all the many colour mutations. Crested Zebra Finches will not appeal to all breeders but like other Crested varieties they will have a number of interested supporters. Crests will certainly add a further dimension to the exhibiting side of the fast growing Zebra Finch Fancy.

It will be understood that at the present time the number of these Crested Zebra Finches is limited: likewise records of their breeding behaviour. From data already to hand it appears they are following the main principles of inheritance as do other Crested varieties of domesticated mutations. When a Crested bird is paired to a non Crested one, some of their young also have crests which may vary somewhat in their size and shape. The fact that Crests do appear from the first cross shows clearly that the mutation is a Dominant. It would seem that the actual quality of the crest itself is controlled to some extent by the presence of modifiers in the birds' genetical makeup. In addition, selection by the breeder helps considerably to induce pairs to breed birds with the desired shape of crests.

Non Crested birds bred from one Crested parent are known in the bird world as Crestbreds and when paired back to actual Crested birds have the potential of producing more and better Crested types. Bearing this fact in mind breeders of the Crested varieties of birds invariably mate Crest to Crestbred with the most satisfactory results. This type of mating undoubtedly allows the modifiers to arrange themselves so that the better shaped crests result. If improvement in type, substance and general quality is needed then the breeder must use the pure Normal to Crest mating which gives better birds but fewer with crests.

To date there is no evidence that when two Crested birds are mated together a lethal factor comes into play like with the Crested Canary varieties. Nevertheless this possibility should always be borne in mind when making up breeding pairs to produce Crested young. If breeders are improving their stock the question of Crest to Crest mating in Zebra Finches is unlikely to occur for some long time to come and this I feel is a very good thing for the breed.

Breeders should note that the Grey Zebra Finch and all its mutant colours are white ground birds and therefore they can only appear in certain colour shades. Unless there is a very drastic mutation it will not be possible to produce a yellow ground Zebra Finch with yellow or green shades of colour. The only other possibility of getting yellow ground is through the use of a fertile hybrid possessing the necessary colour character. In this area the difficulty is that the majority of suitable birds for cross pairing are also of the white ground kind.

Crested

Chapter 5

The Sex-linked
Colour Mutations

With the majority of domesticated breeds of birds when mutations
occur some of the genetic changes are inherited in a different pattern
to either the more usual Dominant or Recessive kinds. This method
of reproduction is known as Sex-linked because of the particular
characters that cause the mutation are situated on the special pair
of Chromosomes that also determined the sex of the bird. Breeders
are often mystified by the Sex-linked inheritance until they have
mastered the formula which causes this method of inheritance. For
the many intending or new Zebra Finch breeders I will explain why
certain characters are inherited in this particular manner.

All colour and other features are passed from the parent birds to
their young through microscopic bodies known as Chromosomes on
which are even smaller ones called Genes carrying the characters.
The parent birds each have many pairs of Chromosomes in their
genetical makeup all of which are of the same sized pairs except one
pair where one is longer than the other. This special pair controls
the sex, the smaller one is known as Y and the larger one as X and
any bird having a Y in its makeup must be a hen. Therefore the sex
determining Chromosome pair of a hen can be described as XY
and that of a cock as XX. Colour characters can only be carried on
the X and when a hen has a colour character on the single X she
possesses that colour must show in her plumage. Characters carried
on the X Chromosomes are Recessive and because a hen has only
one X on which Chromosomes can be carried such characters appear
to act as Dominant in the case of hens. A cock bird having the
character on only one of his two XXs will not show the colour in
its plumage he must have the character on both of the X pair to do
so. It is possible for more than one colour character to be carried
on an X Chromosome.

When breeders first come across Sex-linkage in their birds they
find the breeding results somewhat puzzling until they realise that
the sex of the bird used plays an important part in the transmission
of colour. At the present time there are three known Sex-linked
colour characters in Zebra Finches, the Fawn, the Albino and the

The chromosome make-up of birds differs from most other animals because the Hen carries the YX chromosome and the Cock has the XX chromosome

The colour character can be carried by the X chromosome only

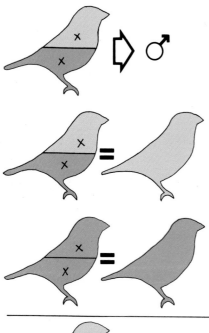

Where only one X chromosome carries the colour character, the colour is "Recessive" and will not show in the plumage

When both X chromosomes carry the same colour character, the colour is shown in the plumage

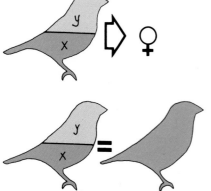

Hens can carry a colour character in their only X chromosome. This will make their colour "Recessive" but as this is the only colour character, it must show in their plumage colouring

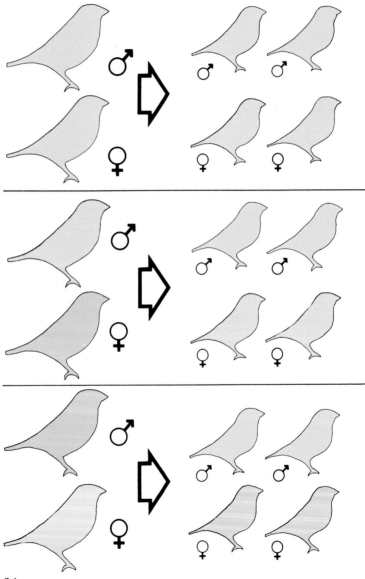

34

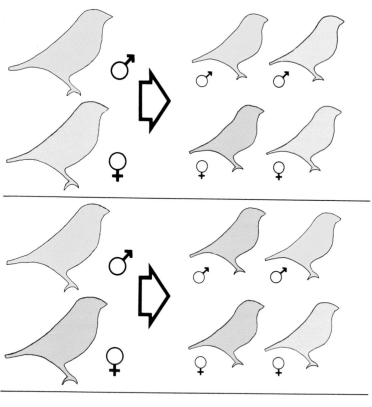

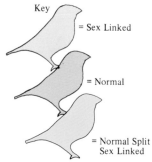

Key

= Sex Linked

= Normal

= Normal Split
  Sex Linked

35

Chestnut-flanked White. It is always possible with new mutations for further Sex-linked characters to appear.

To make Sex-linked inheritance more easy to understand I will give the rules that cover all matings followed by a few actual theoretical expectations.

Sex-linked inheritance

1 Sex-linked cock to Sex-linked hen give 100% Sex-linked cocks and hens.

2 Sex-linked cock to Normal hen gives 50% Normal/Sex-linked cocks and 50% Sex-linked hens.

3 Sex-linked hen to Normal cock gives 50% Normal/Sex-linked cocks and 50% Normal hens.

4 Normal/Sex-linked cock to Sex-linked hen gives 25% Normal/Sex-linked cocks, 25% Sex-linked cocks, 25% Normal hens and 25% Sex-linked hens.

5 Normal/Sex-linked cock to Normal hen gives 25% Normal hens, 25% Sex-linked hens, 25% Normal cocks and 25% Normal/Sex-linked cocks.

When two different kinds of Sex-linked birds are paired together one acts as though it were a Normal.

The two most frequently met with pairings are Nos. 4 and 5. An example of No. 4 is Normal Grey/Fawn cock to Fawn hen which produces Normal Grey/Fawn cocks, Normal Grey hens and Fawn cocks and hens, and No. 5 Normal Grey/Fawn cock to Normal Grey hen gives Normal Grey cocks and hens, Normal Grey/Fawn cocks and Fawn hens. The number of each genetical kind will be found to vary with each individual nest but taken collectively the percentages work out accurately.

It should be remembered when making pairings that it is *not* possible for any *hen* bird to be 'split' for a sex-linked character because if a hen has such a character in her genetical makeup then it must show in her plumage. I specially mention this fact because if a breeder has previously only dealt with recessive colours it would be quite easy to make the mistake of thinking all birds can be 'split', even the sex-linked varieties when they are new to a stock. Of the two sex-linked colour shades that are bred extensively the soft coloured Fawn seems to have the greatest appeal both as aviary and exhibition birds.

A sample case of the Sex-Link principles.

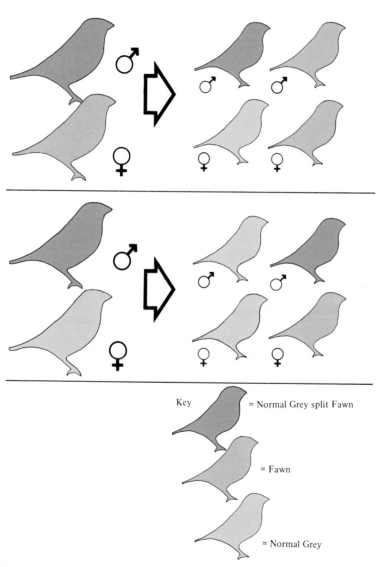

Key = Normal Grey split Fawn

= Fawn

= Normal Grey

37

Fawn
Colour description
Cock Beak: bright coral red. Top of head: rich fawn with each feather edged with darker fawn. Back of neck: fawn. Large ear patches deep orange (varying in depth to correspond with the shade of the overall colour) with a blackish line running from the eyes down one side, this blackish line is followed by a wider white stripe and the beak side is edged with a further thin blackish line. Throat and upper chest: finely barred with blackish-brown and white terminating with a blackish-brown bar about one eighth of an inch (3 mm) wide right across the chest from flank to flank. Lower chest, abdomen and under tail coverts: white but there may be some fawnish shading towards the vent. Flanks: bright chestnut heavily spotted with round white dots. Back: fawn, flights and secondaries fawn slightly duller in tone, rump white merging to blackish-brown and white at sides. Central tail feathers white, widely barred with dark fawn, outer tail feathers blackish-fawn. Iris: red brown to brown. Feet and legs: pinkish.
Hen Beak: orange red. General colouring same as cock except the colour of the ear patches is absent and the breast and flanks are pale fawn instead of the striping and flank markings.

The history of the Fawn mutation is most interesting as the original birds were discovered in the late nineteen twenties flying wild in their native habitat in Australia. In a 1958 Issue of the Avicultural Society of Australia's magazine an account of the catching of the first Fawn Zebra Finches is clearly given. The two original birds were first noted flying in a large flock of Normal Greys around the warm ashes of camp fires. Australia, like many other countries which have high day-time temperatures, have very low temperatures at night and early morning. Zebra Finches being clever little birds have discovered that the remains of camp fires are ideal places to warm up for the day. Apparently these two strangely coloured Zebra Finches were seen by someone interested in birds and plans were made to trap them. After having trapped many hundreds of Normal Greys the two odd coloured specimens were eventually caught and sent to a breeder in Adelaide. The first young bred from these two Fawn hens were naturally normally coloured and it was not until the second generation that other Fawns appeared. It was not known at that time that this new colour followed a sex-linked manner of inheritance. From all accounts the first young Fawns were of poor colour and it took a number of years of careful selective breeding to produce the delightful shade of fawn we know to-day.

Fawn

39

This information from Australia disproved the thought that Fawns originated in South Africa as when this claim was investigated it was found that the South African birds had been bred from Australian stock.

The exact date when Fawns first arrived in Great Britain is not certain but they were mentioned in the 1953 Year Book of The Zebra Finch Society. This means they must have been known here as a separate colour variety some years before that date. Strangely enough two kinds were mentioned at that time – the Fawns and the Cinnamons most probably due to the fact that light and darker coloured birds existed. If this point is examined it will be seen that different shades could be expected in line with the various tones of the Normal Greys. However it did not take long for breeders to discover that the different shades were all due to one mutation. Eventually the name Cinnamon was dropped in favour of Fawn, where both light and dark forms are recognised. Generally speaking the name Cinnamon is given to birds of the yellow ground colour, whereas Fawn is used to denote those with the white ground.

In spite of the competition from other newer colour forms, the Fawns kept a steady place in their popularity amongst breeders for may years. At the present time they are at their peak and there are more Fawns about in breeders' aviaries than any other single colour. Because they possess fine feather quality, and are of good type and substance. Fawns are very frequently used to improve other colours. Although such outcrosses undoubtedly improve other colours, they have a retarding effect on the Fawns themselves. In the production of good quality exhibition strains of Fawns, special care must be taken to ensure that the right type of birds are mated together.

With each Fawn pairing both birds should be selected for their all round quality as well as purity and levelness of colour. The majority of breeders agree that the selected Fawn to selected Fawn gives the best all round result. From the colour angle it is preferable to mate together two birds having the same depth of colour, as this will produce a strain that will produce young of the same level shade. At times a special feature or features need to be introduced into a Fawn strain for the sake of improvement. Whenever possible Normal Greys should be used but this has become much more difficult in recent years because of the shortage of first rate Normal Greys. If the right kind of Normal Greys cannot be obtained then the breeder must use whatever colour can be had with the necessary features. I have seen some very good Fawns that have been bred through Normal Whites or Chestnut-flanked Whites. The main difficulty of using these colours is that the breeder cannot see what colour is being masked by these characters and colour failings can be introduced unseen into a strain by these means.

If the colour of Fawns is assessed at the wrong time it is quite easy to get an incorrect opinion of their shade. It is a well-known fact that all coloured feathers are inclined to fade with age and especially so if they are exposed to strong sunlight and Fawns are particularly susceptible to this fading. The loss of feathers through squabbling or a partial moult can give birds a two tone colour effect and good birds could be discarded for having bad colour. Fawns that are required for exhibition purposes should be allowed to moult in accommodation that does not have long periods of strong sunlight. When being caught or handled every precaution should be taken to prevent feathers being knocked or pulled out. Fawns can be used to produce composite forms and to improve other and new varieties.

Chestnut-flanked White
Colour description
Cock Beak: bright coral red. Top of head: white with slight traces of faint grey on some feather edges. Back of neck: white. Large ear patches orange (varying in depth according to the colour actually being masked by the character) with a blackish line running from the eye down one side, this blackish line is followed by a wider white stripe and the beak side is edged with a further thin blackish line. Throat and upper chest: finely barred with dark grey and white terminating with a dark grey to almost black bar about one eighth of an inch (3 mm) wide right across the chest from flank to flank. Lower chest, abdomen and upper tail coverts white. Flanks: chestnut heavily spotted with round white dots. Back, flights and secondaries white, rump white merging to blackish brown at sides. Central tail feathers white widely barred with blackish-brown, outer tail feathers blackish-brown. Iris: red-brown to brown. Feet and legs: deep reddish pink.

Hen Beak: orange-red to red. General colouring same as cock except the colour of the ear patches is absent. There may be more dark edging to the feathers on front of head than the cock.

I have just described how the first Fawn Zebra Finches were found amongst a wild flock and strangely enough the second sex-linked mutation was also originally found flying in the wild. They were first seen somewhere about 1936/7 in Queensland in company with many wild Greys and were caught and taken into breeding aviaries. Information on these Chestnut-flanked Whites or marked

Whites as they were called is not very full and it has not been stated whether they were cocks and hens or how many birds were first discovered. Being a sex-linked mutation it is most probable that like the Fawns they would have been hens. It did not take long for this most attractive colour form to be established in true breeding stocks, and in due course specimens found their way to other countries where they attracted the attention of many breeders. In addition to being known as Marked Whites in Australia they were also called Marmosettes and Masked Whites in European countries. The latter name appears to have arisen because the young in nest feather have quite a sooty head and mask. When The Zebra Finch Society became the leading Body in the Zebra Finch world the naming of this mutation was fully considered and Chestnut-flanked White was chosen as it met all the necessary requirements. At the present time the name Chestnut-flanked White has been adopted world wide as the correct title for this mutation.

There can be a Chestnut-flanked White form of most of the other mutations but when combined with paler or pied birds the results are not particularly attractive although most intriguing genetically. Undoubtedly the best Chestnut-flanked Whites are those masking Normal Grey or Fawn as the markings of such birds are more clear and distinct. The whole object for breeders of this mutation is to produce specimens that have markings as near as possible to Normals with the overall colour as white as possible. This objective can only be achieved by continuous selection of each parent bird for correctness of colour and show features, the periodic use of good brightly coloured Normals is essential for the continuity of well marked Chestnut-flanked Whites. The inclusion of Normals is Chestnut-flanked White pairings is also important if cheek patch colour is to be maintained as many birds fail in this respect. Individual breeders often have their own ideas as to the best pairings for producing well marked Chestnut-flanked Whites in keeping with their own particular strain of birds. Should any breeder have a special method of pairing I would advise them to continue with such pairings as they obviously are suitable for that particular stock.

During recent years a considerable number of Chestnut-flanked Whites have been bred showing a definite pale cream colour instead of the desired white. It is not known whether these birds owe their existence to a further mutation or are the result of selective breeding from large well made birds that show the tinted colouring. In some lights these shaded birds are very difficult to distinguish from pale Dominant Creams. Although they may be good bold birds I do

Chestnut-flanked White

think breeders should be encouraged to produce Chestnut-flanked Whites that are white in accordance to the Colour Standard of The Zebra Finch Society. If determined efforts are made I feel sure that correctly coloured Chestnut-flanked Whites can once more be developed into strains of bold substantially built birds of good type. I think it would be a great loss to The Zebra Finch Fancy if the original concept of this mutation is allowed to be lost through lack of a combined effort by breeders, exhibitors and judges.

Albino
Colour description
Cock Beak: bright coral red. Top of head right through to tip of tail: pure white. Iris: red. Feet and legs: bright flesh pink.
Hen Beak: lighter red otherwise like cock.

Albinos are the third group known member of the Sex-linked colour group which are quite well known in Australia whereas only a few examples have been seen in Britain and Europe. This form of White differs in three ways from the Normal Whites – their eyes are bright red, they are sex-linked in their breeding behaviour and they do not under any circumstances carry any trace of dark feathers in their plumage.

It would seem that the Australian Albino strains must have occurred in the late nineteen fifties although no precise details are available. It may well have been that in the first instance they were thought to be ordinary Whites and not recognised as Albinos until their breeding behaviour caused them to be examined more closely. At Australian exhibitions Albinos have separate classes which are quite well supported indicating that the variety is being produced in reasonable numbers.

Some years ago I had a report that Albinos were being bred in India and had appeared in a large uncontrolled aviary containing mixed coloured Zebra Finches. These Albinos were said to have been hens and were of poor quality and physique and the strain did not appear to have been established. The most recent news about Albinos came when I was discussing birds with a party of Japanese breeders at the end of last year. Speaking through an interpreter it was difficult to be quite sure if the White birds under discussion were actually Albinos and not White Fawns where the eyes show quite a red gleam at some angles. Nevertheless time will tell as Japanese bird breeders are extremely proficient in developing new types. It is likely to be some years before we shall see any Albino pairs at our exhibitions and then they are likely to have been produced from imported stock. The British and European kinds are likely to be some years before becoming readily available, they are certainly something to look forward to.

Albino

Chapter 6

The Recessive Colour Mutations

In the two previous Chapters I have explained the breeding behaviour of the Dominant and the Sex-linked characters and now
turn to the Recessive kinds which form the largest group. As their
name shows these varieties are just the opposite to the Dominant
kinds and their colour character is only visible when it is carried on
both halves of a chromosome pair. This means that colour characters
can be carried hidden by both cocks and hens. When a bird is
carrying a character in its genetical makeup that is not visible in its
plumage it is said to be 'split' for that character. When such birds
are described their description is written with the visible colour first
followed by an oblique thus '/' and then the hidden colour. As an
example Normal Grey/White shows that the bird's visible colour is
Normal Grey and it carries hidden the character for White which
can be produced by suitable matings as I will explain later. The
chromosome pairs that carry the Recessive colour characters are
different ones from the special sex determining pair mentioned in
the previous Chapter and are of equal size and both capable of
carrying characters. Whatever Recessive characters are carried
either visible or in 'split' form their inheritance is governed by the
following rules.

Recessive inheritance
1 Normal to Recessive gives 100% Normal/Recessive.
2 Normal/Recessive to Normal gives 50% Normal/Recessive and
   50% Normal.
3 Normal/Recessive to Normal/Recessive gives 25% Normal,
   50% Normal/Recessive and 25% Recessive.
4 Normal/Recessive to Recessive gives 50% Normal/Recessive
   and 50% Recessive.
5 Recessive to Recessive gives 100% Recessive.

These rules operate when one Recessive form is being dealt with,
when two different kinds of Recessives are mated together one acts
as a 'Dominant' to the other. The sex of the parent birds has no in-

The Recessive breeding principles

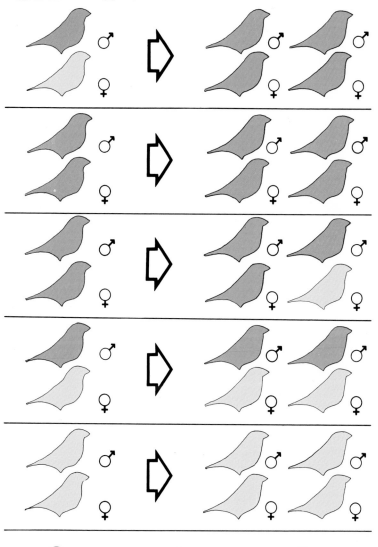

 = Normal

 = Recessive

 = Normal split Recessive

47

fluence on the results of Recessive inheritance. It should be noted that mating No. 3 gives two genetical kinds of normally coloured birds, the difference in these can only be ascertained by test pairings as their visual colour is identical.

White
Colour description
Cock Beak: bright coral red. Top of head right through to tip of tail as pure white as possible. Iris: red brown to brown. Feet and legs: flesh pink.

Hen Beak: lighter red otherwise coloured like cock. Some specimens may show grey or fawn flecking at base of neck and saddle with amounts varying from the odd few flecks to quite a large flecked area. These birds and the pure Whites are all the same genetically with the latter being the result of careful selective breeding.

White is quite a common variation from the natural colour of numerous species of birds and it was the first one to be definitely recorded in Zebra Finches. It is difficult to find out the exact date when White Zebra Finches were first bred but it is known that a strain of Whites were in Sydney, Australia, in 1921. With all probability these were the first Whites to have been bred and undoubtedly were the foundation stock from which our present day Whites were evolved. Information on the actual colour of these original Australian White strain is not available therefore it is not certain whether they were pure in colour or if they carried some grey flecking.

Until the availability of other colour mutations the Whites were much sought after by bird breeders of that time but strangely enough very few found their way on to the show benches. When the Zebra Finch Society began to give support to shows Whites began to emerge as exhibition birds. Since the early nineteen sixties their popularity has fluctuated somewhat although there has always been a steady core of enthusiastic breeders. The highlight of White Zebra Finches as exhibition birds came when a pair won the Supreme Trophy at the National Exhibition of Cage and Aviary Birds in 1972 and were the first Zebra Finches of any colour to gain such an award. This success caused the steady increasing popularity of Zebra Finch keeping, breeding and exhibiting to rise at a much faster rate and now Zebra Finches are being bred all over the world by tens of thousands.

Ordinary White Zebra Finches can be bred quite easily but the production of those with absolutely clear white plumage takes care-

White

ful planning of the breeding pairs. The White character can mask any of the other colour mutations so a White must be a White form of Normal Grey, Fawn, Penguin etc. etc. At the present time the exhibition type Whites appear to be the White forms of either Normal Grey, Fawn or Pied. This being so many odd colours will appear in the nests of White crosses mostly unbeknown to their owners. The best way to start breeding and building up a strain of good pure coloured Whites is first to obtain one or preferably a pair of birds that have little or no flecking visible on their plumage. If the breeder gets an unrelated pair these can both be mated with Fawns as many breeders think the best and clearest birds are the White Fawns. When a Fawn cock is paired to a White masking Normal Grey the resulting young will be Normal Grey/Fawn White cocks and Fawn/White hens. The other mating of White masking Normal Grey cock to Fawn hen gives Normal Grey/Fawn White cocks and Normal Grey/White hens. No actual White birds will come from these crosses unless of course the Fawns happen to be 'split' for White – a possibility that is always present. The following season the breeder can cross pair the young, putting Normal Grey/Fawn White cocks with either Fawn/White or Normal Grey/White hens. From the first pairing a small number of White Fawn cocks and hens will result and from the latter some White Fawn hens. The adult Whites can also be usefully paired to the young from the opposite pair. From all of these pairings any Fawn or White Fawn young that appear can be identified on hatching by the colour of their eyes. The skin covering the eyes of all young birds that are Fawns is pinkish flesh-coloured which stands out quite clearly against the blackish skin colour of the Normals. As the young Fawns develop so their eyes become darker although when viewed at an angle in a good light they always show a reddish gleam. Once the breeder has produced a number of White Fawn birds selected for purity of colour can be mated together. To maintain and improve the strain good quality Fawn/Whites can be introduced periodically and for this purpose first cross 'split' birds are the most useful. Similar pairings as indicated above can be used when Normal Greys or Pieds are used for outcrosses but here of course no sex-linkage is involved. A White Normal Grey paired to a Normal Grey will give Normal Grey/White cocks and hens. Two such birds paired together will give the theoretical expectation of 25% pure Normal Grey, 50% Normal Grey/White and 25% White Normal Grey. If a Pied Normal Grey is used the result would be normal Grey/Pied White and when paired together would give Normal Greys, Pied

Normal Greys, White Pied Normal Greys and White Normal Greys. Whatever coloured birds are used as outcrosses it is essential that a careful selection is made of the White birds when mating them together in the third generation. Whites can be recommended as aviary or exhibition birds both for the beginner and the more experienced breeder.

Pied Normal Grey
Colour description
Cock Beak: coral red. Colouring as Normal Grey with the colours well broken showing about 50% white (the white of the underparts not to be included in the 50%). Characteristic markings on cheeks, chest, flanks and tail to be retained but in a broken form. Tear markings can be either broken or intact.

Hen Beak: lighter red otherwise like cock except the colour of the ear patches are absent and the breast and flanks pale silvery-grey instead of the striping and markings with the pied areas to match pattern of cock. Although the Whites are thought to be the first mutation it is quite within the bounds of possibility that lightly marked Pieds appeared before them but were not recorded, beyond being classed as mismarked birds. Pied Normal Grey Zebra Finches were first reported from Denmark about 1935 and the mutation was quickly established in spite of it being a Recessive one. It was not long before Pieds were being extensively bred in many countries and Pied forms of other mutations were quickly produced by enterprising breeders. To show their colour pattern to its best advantage it is preferable to breed Pied Normal Greys and Pied Fawns. Many of the other Pieds form are far less spectacular although of great genetical interest.

Because of the variability of the colour pattern carried by Pieds it needs that extra special care to be taken in the selection of partners and of the birds used for outcrossing. When outsrocsing, the Pied partners should be chosen for their closeness to the desired standard pattern and the Normal birds for their purity and evenness of overall colouring. The first cross should be selected Pied to selected Normal which will produce 100% Normal/Pied which can be mated together or to other selected Pieds. From the first mating 25% Pieds will result and from the second 50%. It will be realised that the pattern markings of these Pieds may vary considerably but as a series of selected pairings are carried out so the variations tend to become progressively less. When both members of breeding pairs are Pieds the breeder should endeavour to match compensating pattern markings as this tends to give more balanced marked young.

In recent years the Pied Fawns seem to have been bred in greater numbers and the combination of the two colour forms gives a most satisfactory and attractive looking bird. Their production is not quite as simple as the Normal Grey bird because of the inclusion of the sex-linked inheritance of the Fawn character. They can be bred from similar matings as indicated for the production of White Fawns by substituting Pied for White and following the selection method as for Pied Normal Greys.

When exhibiting either Pied Normal Greys and Pied Fawns it is very important to match the pattern markings of the pairs as closely as possible so as to form matched pairs. It will often be found that Pied birds from the same parents will give the best matching exhibition pairs. Related pairs will also provide the exhibitor with good matching birds for show. Although related birds are good for exhibiting their close relationship will make them unsuitable for actual breeding purposes. The colour description for Pied Fawn is the same as for Pied Normal Grey except the colour is Fawn in place of Grey. There are two big colour faults to be watched for when selecting exhibition birds, firstly unbroken markings on cock birds and either light or dark areas of colouring being too extensive on either sex. Birds with such failings will not be good for showing but can be most useful in the breeding quarters when counterbalancing the colour of the breeding pairs.

Penguin
Colour description
Cock Beak: bright coral red. Head, neck, back and wings: soft pale silvery-grey with the flights, secondaries and coverts edged with a paler shade of grey producing a lace-like pattern. The full effect of this lacing is not seen to advantage until after the first and following complete moults. All the underparts from below chin to vent are pure unbroken white. Cheek lobes: pale cream to pale orange to match the actual shade of body colour. Tail: silvery-grey widely barred with white. Flanks: reddish-brown ornamented with clear round white spots. Feet and legs: pinkish. Iris: red brown to brown.

Hen Beak: lighter red otherwise coloured like cock except the colour of the ear patches is white.

At one time this mutation was known by several names such as Silverwings and White-bellies in addition to Penguins. Once again after much careful thought The Zebra Finch Society came to the conclusion that the title of Penguin was much more suitable for this

Normal Pied

mutation. The name is very descriptive and cannot be confused with any of the other mutations as several of them have silvery coloured wings and all have white underparts. It will have been seen from the colour description that Penguins have a definite patterned colouring showing a loss of pattern colour in certain areas.

Their origin is by no means clear beyond the fact they were known to have been breeding in Australia in the nineteen forties. Somewhere about a decade later they were first bred in Europe and a year or two after that examples were being produced in British breeding establishments. The first Penguins seen in Great Britain were smaller and more slender birds than the varieties already being bred and consequently their adoption by breeders was somewhat restricted. The character that is responsible for this mutation is Recessive and their slender shape was closely linked with their colouring. When this happens in a mutation it is always a slow process to break the link and to increase substance and type.

There can be a Penguin form of all the other colour mutations but it is only the Normal Grey and Fawn types that are really attractive. The other combinations give birds that have very diluted colouring and the contrast between the dark and white areas is thereby lost. For the breeders interested in producing composite type of birds they form a most useful addition to the pairings. The actual colour of Penguin Normal Greys and Penguin Fawns is more pallid than their counterparts but this is compensated by the attractive lace-like colouring on their upper parts. Their actual depth of colour may vary a little depending on the shade of the Normals used in their initial production.

I mentioned earlier about the lack of size and the shape of the Penguins originally imported and this means that special attention must be given to pairings that are to breed birds of exhibition quality. A few keen Zebra Finch breeders did take up the Penguin mutation and through their skill and perseverance have now produced strains that are fast approaching the quality of the Normals. Once more the technique of selection and the use of first cross 'split' birds has played a decisive part in their improvement. If the following method of production is carried out Penguins of exhibition substance and type can be bred within a few seasons.

The birds used in all these matings should be the best obtainable for substance, type and colour, as if just ordinary quality birds are used the desired improvement cannot be made. If a pure Normal Grey, the sex does not matter, is paired to a Penguin Normal Grey the result will be 100% Normal Grey/Penguin first cross young.

Penguin

These birds should in turn be mated with selected Penguin Normal Greys and will produce 50% Penguin Normal Greys and 50% Normal Grey/Penguins. Penguin Normal Greys from such pairings invariably show a slight improvement in overall quality and should be mated to further selected first cross 'splits'. This second first cross 'split' pairing should give young Penguins showing a greater improvement and if this process is followed for several seasons the result will be most satisfactory. A few nice quality Penguins can be obtained by the crossing together of two first cross 'split' birds. When two such birds are mated together they will give the theoretical expectation of 25% pure Normal Grey, 50% Normal Grey/Penguins and 25% Penguin Normal Greys. However such pairings are often considered by breeders to be somewhat wasteful as they produce 75% young whose genetical makeup cannot be ascertained except by test pairings. This is of course true to some extent but the quality of any Penguins bred will amply compensate the breeder for the 'wastage'.

The other Penguin form which is gaining many enthusiastic breeders is the Penguin Fawn which has a most pleasing warm shade of colour. It will be realised that they are a little more difficult to breed in the first instance because of the sex-linkage of the Fawn character. This point makes them even more interesting to produce than the Normal Grey kind. Because of the sex-linked inheritance of the Fawn character it is best if it can be so arranged to use Fawn cocks as mates for Penguin Normal Grey hens. The theoretical expectation for this cross is 50% Normal Grey/Penguin Fawn cocks and 50% Fawn/Penguin hens. The Normal Grey/Penguin Fawn cocks can be mated to Fawn/Penguin hens and amongst their young will be numbers of both Penguin Fawn and Penguin Normal Grey cocks and hens. After a number of Penguin Fawns have been bred they can be paired with Fawns so that in the first generation all the young they breed will be of the Fawn kind. The theoretical expectation of the Fawn/Penguin to Penguin Fawn is Fawn/Penguin cocks and hens and Penguin Fawn cocks and hens. The same selection of the breeding pairs should be made as for the Penguin Normal Grey. Special care must be taken at all times to avoid the use of Penguin cocks that show traces of barring on their throat and chest. If this is not watched for the colour pattern will quickly deteriorate and their attraction lost.

Recessive Silver

Recessive Silver (Dilute Normal Grey)
Colour description
Cock Beak: coral red. Top of head: medium silver-grey with each feather edged with darker silver-grey. Back of neck: silver-grey. Large ear patches pale orange to reddish-orange with a blackish line running from the eyes down one side, this blackish line is followed by a wider white stripe and the beak side is edged with a further thin blackish line. Throat and upper chest: finely barred with sooty grey to grey and white terminating with a sooty grey bar about one eighth of an inch (3 mm) wide right across the chest from flank to flank. Lower chest, abdomen and under tail coverts white. Flanks: chestnut, heavily spotted with round white dots. Back, flights and secondaries: medium silver grey, rump white merging to blackish and white at sides. Central tail feathers white widely barred with blackish grey, outer tail feathers slightly darker. Iris: red brown to brown. Feet and legs: pinkish to light orange.
Hen Beak: reddish-orange. General colouring same as cock except that light ear patches may show. Breast and flanks: pale silver-grey instead of striping and flanking markings.

From what information is available it would appear that the Recessive Silver mutation was first discovered breeding in Denmark. At this same period the Dominant Silvers were being bred in Australian aviaries and the two breeding kinds were undoubtedly confused with each other making identification more difficult. Several strains of this Recessive kind were established in Europe and selective breeding took place in certain aviaries and developed variations in shades of colour with one having a more bluish tone. These blue-grey birds were named by their breeders as 'Blues' and specimens were imported into Great Britain under that name. This led to a certain amount of confusion amongst breeders as to the inheritance of Silvers, some thinking them Dominant and others Recessive. In actual fact there were two kinds – the Dominant Australian Silvers and the Recessive Danish Silvers (including the so-called 'Blues'). In due course the two breeding kinds were sorted out so that the breeding pairs eventually put up were birds of the same kind. The cases where crossing had taken place soon evolved themselves with the Dominant kind eliminating the Recessive.

For a short period of time a number of British Zebra Finch breeders became interested in producing Recessive Silvers and some very nicely coloured examples were bred. On the whole Recessive Silvers are much deeper in their overall colour than the Dominant Silvers but their colouring always tends to be more even in tone.

There are varying shades of Recessive Silvers due to the different shades of the Normal Greys from which they were evolved. Recessive Silvers never had much chance of becoming really popular in face of the strong competition from the Dominant Silvers which are so much easier to breed and improve. At the present time they are more widely known in Europe than in Great Britain so that many strains will undoubtedly be kept alive.

Being a Recessive mutation the character can be handed down unseen for many generations and exists in the genetical makeup of numerous birds in our aviaries at the present time. This is borne out by the fact that periodically I hear about Silvers appearing in nests from two normally coloured parents. On investigation these Silvers have always turned out to be members of the Recessive group.

A Normal Grey/Recessive Silver when paired to a Normal Grey will give 50% of each genetical kind and this can go on until two 'split' birds happen to become mated together. The theoretical expectation from Normal Grey/Recessive Silver to Normal Grey/Recessive Silver is 25% pure Normal Grey, 50% Normal Grey/Recessive Silver and 25% Recessive Silver. When two Recessive Silvers are paired together all their young are Recessive Silvers.

Recessive Cream (Dilute Fawn)
Colour description
Cock Beak: coral red. Top of head: medium cream with each feather edged with dark cream. Back of neck: medium cream. Large ear patches reddish-orange (varying in depth to correspond with the shade of the overall colour) with a blackish line running from the eyes down one side, this blackish line is followed by a wider white stripe and the beak side is edged with a further blackish line. Throat and upper chest: finely barred with sooty brown and white terminating with a sooty brown bar about one eighth of an inch (3 mm) wide right across the chest from flank to flank. Lower chest, abdomen and under tail coverts: white but there may be some cream shading towards the vent. Flanks: chestnut, heavily spotted with round white dots. Back: medium cream, flights and secondaries somewhat duller in tone, rump white merging to sooty brown and white at sides. Central tail feathers white, widely barred with dark brown, other tail feathers slightly darker. Iris: red-brown to brown. Feet and legs: pinkish.

Hen Beak: reddish-orange. General colouring same as cock except the colour of the ear patches is absent and the breast and flanks are cream instead of the striping and flank markings.

As it would be expected the Recessive Creams are the direct result of combining the Recessive Silver character with the Sex-linked Fawn. By crossing Fawn cocks with Recessive Silver hens the resulting young are Normal Grey/Fawn Recessive Cream cocks and Fawn/Recessive Cream hens. No actual cream coloured birds appear in the first generation from these crosses although there are Fawn hens. The next pairings of Normal Grey/Fawn Recessive Cream cocks to Fawn/Recessive Cream hens will give a percentage of the desired Recessive Cream cocks and hens. Subsequent matings of Recessive Cream cocks to Fawn/Recessive hens will give 50% Fawn/ Recessive Cream cocks and hens and 50% Recessive Cream cocks and hens. Fawns of medium colour intensity are best used for the production of Recessive Cream as if the very light Fawns are used it is often quite difficult to distinguish between the light Fawns and Recessive Creams.

Other Recessive Cream mutations have been reported both in Great Britain and in Europe but as far as I can gather strains of these birds have not been established. The mutations may have been lost through crossing them with the already established Recessive Creams derived from the Fawns. One particular mutation I saw had a nice warm medium colour throughout, with the secondaries edged with a very definite reddish fawn which have a most pleasing colour effect. The Recessive Silver and Cream mutation could certainly do with some keen Fanciers to take them up once again and put them well on the Zebra Finch Fancy map.

Yellow-beak
Colour description
Cock Beak: deep yellow to orange-yellow. General colouring and markings approximately the same as the descriptions already given for other mutations. The colouring may be a little less bright than that of the red-beaked kind.

Hen Beak: yellow. General colouring same as for other hens except the colour is less bright.

It is difficult to trace just when the Yellow-beak forms came into being as the mutation was not recognised as such for a number of years after it was first seen. The very first live examples I saw were about 1954–1955 in two places in the Midlands and these birds were in their Grey and Fawn kinds. Originally the beak colour was put down to the birds being just poorly coloured and for this reason were mostly discarded from breeding quarters. The consequence of this was that these birds were only bred unintentionally and their

Recessive Cream

numbers were very small. After a considerable period of time it was suddenly realised that the Yellow-beak was a mutation and could be had in all the other colour mutations. In 1972 The Zebra Finch Society recognised the mutation and all the Yellow-beak kinds then became established.

The Yellow-beak character is a Recessive one and reproduces just like all the other Recessive mutations. A Yellow-beaked bird paired to any Red-beaked variety will give only red-beaked young all of which carry the Yellow-beak character. When two Red-beaked/Yellow-beaked are paired together they give the theoretical expectation of 25% pure Red-beaked, 50% Red-beaked/Yellow-beaked and 25% Yellow-beaked and it is from such matings that the majority of the Yellow-beaked birds have been produced. At first most Yellow-beaked birds appeared unexpectedly in nests of normally coloured beaked birds usually to the complete surprise of the breeder. Since their recognition by The Zebra Finch Society a few breeders have now set themselves the task of improving the mutation from an exhibition angle and have made special pairings with this in mind. I think that the Yellow-beaks will add something extra to the shows and they can be bred side by side with their normal counterparts without causing the breeder any difficulty.

The mutations I shall be describing in the following paragraphs have not up to the present time been officially named or recognised by The Zebra Finch Society. Although some of these forms are now breeding quite freely in European aviaries they are not yet being bred in Great Britain although some examples do exist. It should not be long now before we shall be seeing some of these new colours on the show benches and their appearance should add further to the spread of keeping Zebra Finches.

Light-back
Colour description
Cock Beak: coral red. Top of head: silver with each feather edged with dark silver. Large ear patches light orange brown with a blackish line running from down one side. This blackish line is followed by a wider white stripe and the beak side is edged with a further thin blackish line. Throat and upper chest: finely barred black and white terminating in a black bar about one eighth of an inch (3 mm) wide right across the chest from flank to flank. Lower chest, abdomen and under tail coverts: white. Flanks: light chestnut heavily spotted with round white dots. Back, flights and secondaries light silver, rump white merging to black and white at sides. Central

Yellow-beak White

tail feathers white widely barred with black, outer tail feathers black. Iris: red-brown to brown. Feet and legs: deep pink.

Hen Beak: red orange. General colouring same as cock except the colour of ear patches is absent. Breast and flanks: light silver instead of the striping and flanking markings.

Precise details of the arrival of this mutation seem to be non existent although they have been bred for quite a number of years now. It was Prof. H. Steiner of Zurich, Switzerland, who first discovered the mutation in a mixed batch of Normal Zebra Finches. In the experiments he carried out Prof. Steiner established the fact that they were actually a separate variety and not a lighter form of an older one. They are thought to be Recessive in their manner of inheritance but this has to be checked out by breeding experiments.

Light-backs are rather handsome with their half depth of even normal colour on the upper part of their body but still retaining the full black colour on throat, breast and tail. They are now called Light-Backs on the Continent but most probably their name may be altered when more details of the mutation are available for examination. When specimens become available for breeders in this country and they are bred to our exhibition standards I feel certain they will quickly become a popular exhibition and aviary Colour. I hope to have more details about these birds in a few seasons as I have two examples now in my aviaries which are about to start breeding operations.

Saddle-back
Colour description
Cock Coloured as Normal White except for a patch (saddle) of grey or fawn on base of neck and over shoulders. The extent of this dark area can vary.

Hen Coloured as Normal White except for a patch (saddle) of grey or fawn on the back.

Reports about these birds are many and varied with the present consensus of opinion being that they are heavily flecked Normal Whites. These flecked birds do appear in nests where Whites are breeding in mixed communities and quite a number of aviary owners have reported their appearance. If a series of selective matings were carried out with the most heavily flecked stock it is very possible that a Saddle-back form that was true breeding could be evolved. On the other hand there may exist quite a separate mutation giving the Saddle-back pattern and it may have been eclipsed by the presence of the heavily flecked White form. The position can only be

Black-breasted Zebra Finch

satisfactorily evolved by a series of test pairings when examples become available for this purpose.

Black-breasted
Colour description

Cock Beak: coral red. Top of head: grey with each feather edged with darker grey. Ear patches quite extensive and of a bright orange brown without the black line from the eyes down one side. The ear patches are followed by a wide white stripe which is edged on the beak side by a thin black line. Throat and upper chest: solid black with a few white marks near flanks. Lower chest, abdomen and under tail coverts: tinted white. Flanks: chestnut, heavily marked with oblong white marks. Back, flights and secondaries grey with some brownish edging to the feathers. Rump: white. Central tail feathers: beige with some black marks, outer feathers: black. Iris: red brown. Feet and legs: deep reddish-pink.

Hen Beak: red orange. General colouring same as cock except the large ear patches are pale silver-grey. Upper throat: beige, breast: grey, abdomen and under tail coverts: grey. Flankings are absent.

Many Zebra Finch breeders have heard of Black-breasted Zebra Finches but few in Great Britain have actually seen live specimens. In Europe they are quite widely bred and generally called by their German name Schwarsbrust and in Australia where a similar mutation exists they are known as Black-faced or Black-fronted. Although there is scant information available about the Australian kind, what there is points strongly to the fact that the two forms may be one and the same mutation. The genetical behaviour of both the German and the Australian kinds is still far from being clear and more experimental pairings are needed before it will be solved. From the few breeding results that have filtered through it looks as though the Black-breasted character may well be a Dominant one. Such an assumption is quite feasible as birds having a predominance of black in their plumage are always likely to be Dominant over paler shades.

The colour pattern of the Black-breasted is quite different from that of any of the other mutations that have so far appeared and in actual colouring they have new shades. Information received from European breeders shows that the Black-breasted and particularly cock birds have a much shorter life than other Zebra Finch colour forms. This feature may be due to the European birds all being evolved from a strain having this drawback and that in time when crossed out to more vigorous types it may be eliminated. I certainly hope that this will prove to be correct as Black-breasted are a most pleasing addition to our growing list of Zebra Finch colour mutations.

Black
At the present time no breeding strains of wholly black Zebra Finches exist although completely black and partially black specimens are bred from time to time. In nest feather and first adult feather the cock birds are completely black with very dark chestnut ear patches and flank markings with the latter being devoid of the characteristic white dots. Other specimens have dark grey plumage with large areas of black on back, wings, chest, and again very dark chestnut ear patches and flankings minus the white dots. The strange thing about these melanistic birds is that they either die when a few months old or moult out into dark greys with perhaps the odd black feather. Young produced by these 'black' birds have so far all been normally coloured so it would appear that their colouring is physical and not genetic.

A further black feather carrying kind is breeding in Europe and are called Schwarzling. These birds are similar to Normal Greys only of a darker shade with black on upper chest, back of neck, flights wing butts and where the legs join the body. The flank markings are chestnut with only a very few white dots. Here again the details of their breeding behaviour is somewhat obscure.

Grizzle
Colour description
Cock Beak: coral red. General colour as for Normal Grey with all the dark areas quite heavily flecked with white giving a grizzled or pepper and salt effect. Iris: red brown. Feet and legs: deep pink.
Hen Same as cock except colour of ear patches is absent. Chest markings and flank markings absent. This mutation is yet another that has first occurred in Australia and only a very few specimens have actually been seen out of that country. The grizzle colour effect is not unexpected as in many domesticated species of birds it does occur regularly. Owing to the lack of breeding material it has not yet been possible to solve the hereditary nature of these birds in this country. From Australian information it would seem that the mutation may well be a further Recessive one. No doubt in due course when birds become available for experiments it will be unravelled.

Other Colour possibilities

Over the past twenty to twenty five years odd specimens have been bred with differently coloured plumage or pattern to those already known. In all instances these colour breaks were not established but of course it is always possible for them to recur and to be developed under more favourable circumstances. With the big spread of Zebra Finch breeding all over the world new colours are likely to occur and breeders are advised to watch out for any unusually coloured birds that may occur in the nests.

Zebra Finches are white ground birds and it seems most unlikely that a yellow ground could appear as a mutation but it could happen through the use of a fertile hybrid having the necessary colour in its makeup. Over the years numbers of Zebra Finch hybrids have actually been produced mostly with members of the Mannikin family as one of the parents. If a yellow ground Zebra Finch could be produced the number of colours would automatically be doubled. It will be interesting to see what some enterprising breeder will achieve in this direction.

Chapter 7

Accommodation

Because of their ability to breed very well in comparatively small quarters Zebra Finches have found favour with modern bird keepers who find birdroom and aviary space something of a problem. Zebra Finches can be kept and successfully bred in a wide range of structures from purpose built birdrooms and aviaries to all kinds of other buildings that have been adapted for the purpose. Although they are only quite small birds they should not be subjected to living in overcrowded or cramped accommodation. In the following paragraphs I shall be describing some of the types of housing most frequently used by Zebra Finch breeders for their birds.

Undoubtedly cages are the most convenient way for housing Zebra Finches if they are to be bred under complete control both for exhibition and colour breeding. Cages either in single units or in blocks can be fitted into garden sheds, garages, birdrooms or a spare room in the house. To obtain the best overall results the cages should not be less than say 3′ (1 m) in length by 1½′ (·5 m) high and about 15″ (·4 m) in depth. The actual measurements of single cages or blocks can be adjusted so they will fit comfortably in to the space that is available. Cage fronts made of punch bars as used for Budgerigar cages are most suitable and can be bought at Bird Stores. These fronts are in a variety of sizes and most have a large door which is useful for putting in nest boxes, cleaning out the cages, and for ringing young birds. The materials used for the box part of the cages can be wooden boards, plywood, various manufactured wood and cardboards or a mixture of these materials. To get the maximum amount of light the cages can be decorated both inside and outside with white emulsion paint or some good brand of non lead containing paint. It is essential that all painted work is thoroughly dry and hard before the birds are given access to the cages. Cages of the size mentioned above will be suitable for housing one breeding pair, four to six birds being steadied for show work, or up to ten non breeding birds.

When cages are constructed in tiered blocks it is advantageous to separate the cages by moveable wooden partitions so that when needed several can be thrown together by simply taking out the partitions. This will give the owner a number of nice long flights

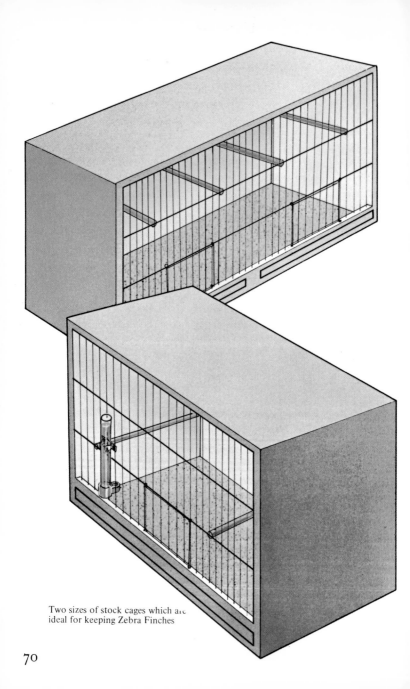

Two sizes of stock cages which are ideal for keeping Zebra Finches

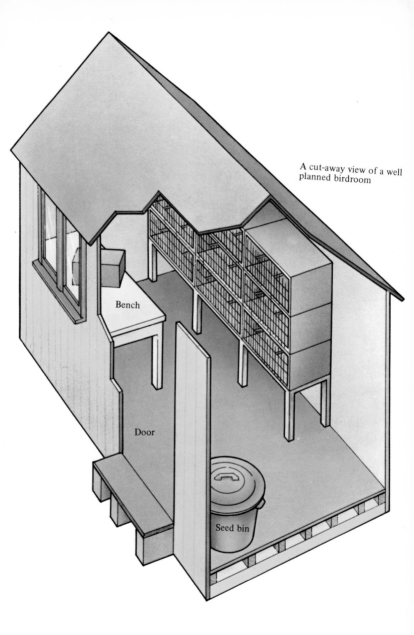

A cut-away view of a well planned birdroom

Bench

Door

Seed bin

71

where the birds can be kept during the non breeding season. Cage flights such as these will be valuable if the breeder has not the space to construct separate flights.

Most strains of Zebra Finches will breed quite well in cages but experience has shown that breeding results in pens or aviaries are usually even more satisfactory. To have such accommodation it means that the breeding establishment will take up considerably more space for the same number of breeding pairs as would cages. Pens can be built in series with or without outside flights and their size adjusted to fit in with the available space. A good practical size for pens is 4' 6" (1·5 m) in length by 6' 6" (2 m) high and about 2' 6" (·66 m) wide. If outside flights are to be attached to these pens they can be made of a size to suit the breeder's own requirements. Pens of this size will accommodate one or two breeding pairs or about two dozen non breeding adults or young. Materials used for building pens are small mesh wire netting and light wooden battens and it is best if these are made in sections so they can be put up or moved according to requirements. Pens can be constructed in the same kind of buildings as for cages and it is usual to decorate all the woodwork with white emulsion paint and to put sand or fine gravel on the floor.

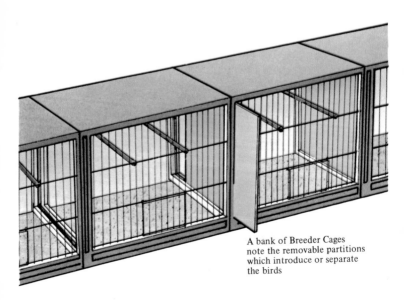

A bank of Breeder Cages
note the removable partitions
which introduce or separate
the birds

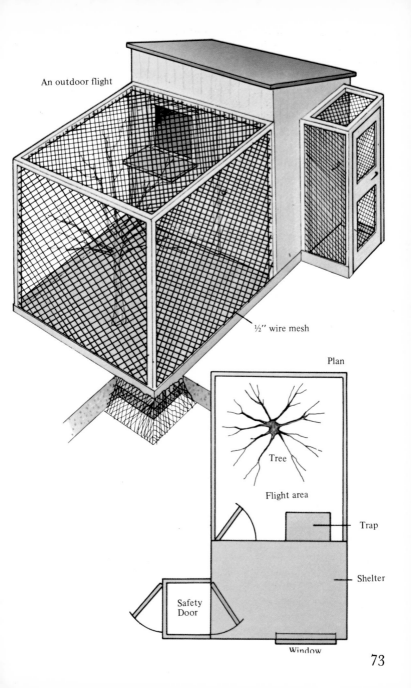

An outdoor flight

½" wire mesh

Plan

Tree

Flight area

Trap

Shelter

Safety
Door

Window

73

Aviaries, particularly flighted ones, are the best for housing Zebra Finches as these buildings are more decorative and the birds can be seen to greater advantage. Of course with aviary breeding the owner has no control over the breeding pairs and consequently this method is not the most suitable for those who wish to breed exhibition stock or develop colours. Nevertheless flighted garden aviaries of mixed coloured Zebra Finches will give a great deal of pleasure and the birds themselves will appreciate the freedom and reproduce freely. Because of the lack of control of the breeding stock they will need to be changed or supplemented periodically so as to prevent undue inbreeding and its accruing deterioration of the stock. However if the pairs are matched and kept in single pair cages for a week or two before putting them out into the aviary most of the pairs will keep together.

It is general practice when constructing outdoor flighted aviaries to have the flight section approximately twice as long as the shelter. Here again there are no hard and fast rules about size or shape and individual breeders can adjust to suit their own special requirements. The floor of the shelter can be boarded, concreted or covered with stone slabs with all precautions being taken against the intrusion of vermin particularly mice. Any of these floors should be covered with coarse sawdust, washed sand, fine gravel or a mixture of these materials.

The floor of the outdoor flight can be covered with various grasses, gravel and some bushes or shrubs planted both for shelter and decoration. Perches in the shelter and the flight can be made of machined wooden dowelling or branches from fruit and similar trees. Stone or brickwork banks and a shallow bathing pool can be added if desired as these all help to make a planted flighted aviary more interesting and attractive. Before any new structure is erected it is advisable to enquire at the local authority offices to see if there are any special requirements governing garden buildings. I mention this fact as regulations regarding buildings vary in different parts of the country.

For holding the birds seeds, grits and water, in all kinds of accommodation, it is preferable to use shallow flat vessels made of earthenware, glass, plastic or metal. In the case of larger aviaries seed hoppers and drinking water fountains will be found easier to cope with. Shallow containers of water for bathing should also be supplied. Care should be taken to make certain that all vessels are placed so they are not contaminated by the droppings of the birds from perches or nest boxes. In aviaries wall shelves or small centrally placed tables will be found most practical and in pens and cages the

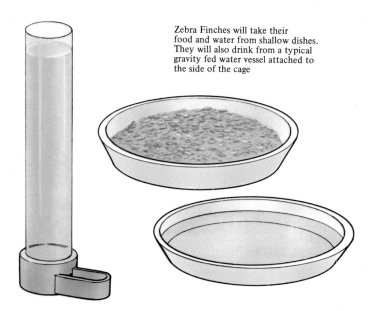

Zebra Finches will take their
food and water from shallow dishes.
They will also drink from a typical
gravity fed water vessel attached to
the side of the cage

containers are mostly placed on the floor.

Perches used for cages, pens or aviaries, should be of varying thicknesses so that the feet and legs of the birds do not get stiff through lack of movement. In this connection the natural tree branches are of great value as they give the birds a constant variation in foot grip. As Zebra Finches do not gnaw woodwork like Budgerigars many more kinds of branches can safely be used for their perching.

Chapter 8

Feeding and foods

The diet required for keeping Zebra Finches in a healthy condition is very simple and straightforward as their diet mainly comprises various seeds which can be given either in separate dishes or blended into a mixture. Small yellow millet seed, commonly known as panicum millet, form the bulk of the mixtures and added to this is white millet, Japanese millet, plate yellow millet and small canary seed in varying quantities. I have found that a good mixture can be made up from blending two parts plate yellow millet, one part each of white millet, Japanese millet, and small canary seed with four parts of panicum millet. Such a mixture can be used throughout the year and in cold weather small quantities of oil containing seeds such as niger and linseed can usefully be added. The amount of the oil containing seeds offered must always be controlled and limited as if eaten in quantity will be very fattening and any benefits otherwise gained will be lost. Some birds will eat certain quantities of the

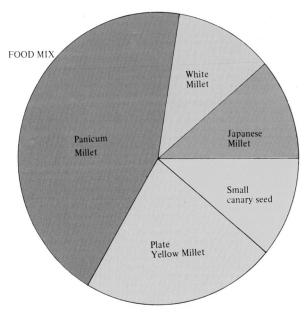

FOOD MIX

White Millet

Japanese Millet

Panicum Millet

Small canary seed

Plate Yellow Millet

seeds contained in wild seed mixture and will derive extra vitamins from doing so. It is best to offer a wide variety of seeds to Zebra Finches whilst they are quite young as adult birds have very firm ideas as to their likes and dislikes.

A very favourite food with Zebra Finches is small yellow millet in the ears and these are generally known as millet sprays. Most breeders give these sprays in their dry state but they can also be offered after having been soaked in cold water. The sprays needed are completely submerged in water for some twenty four hours, then taken out and when the surplus water is shaken off they are ready for the birds. Soaked sprays are useful when green food is scarce and also when chicks are in the nests.

At breeding times the birds will much appreciate some form of soft food and most breeders have their own ideas as to the form that the soft food should take. One of the canary soft foods mixed as directed will be eaten by the majority of Zebra Finches as will a mixture of equal parts of a canary soft food and a fine insectivorous mixture. Some breeders use bread and milk when the birds have young and also as an addition to the diet during moulting periods. Another food used quite extensively is wholemeal bread either moistened with cold water or a weak mixture of honey and water. To help breeding pairs with the feeding of their growing young it is advisable to give them some kind of soft food in addition to their usual seeds. Individual pairs and different strains of birds have their own special favourite kind of soft food therefore if one sort is refused others should be tried until the right one is found. During winter months and in the show season an occasional dish of the birds' favourite soft food will be found most beneficial in helping them to retain their condition. Whenever soft food is used any that remains uneaten at the end of the day should be removed. Stale or mouldy soft food will quickly cause stomach trouble which can have drastic consequences to the health of the birds.

After many years of breeding all kinds of birds I have found that the regular use of green food plays an essential part in keeping birds in a vigorous healthy state. Zebra Finches are extremely fond of many different kinds of green foods and it is therefore possible to give them a supply right through the year. At breeding times when young are in the nest they will eat much larger amounts and the young undoubtedly benefit from the fresh vitamins they receive. Although Zebra Finches will eat a great variety of greens their favourites appear to be chickweed, seeding grasses and spinach, in that order. These green foods are obtainable for quite long periods

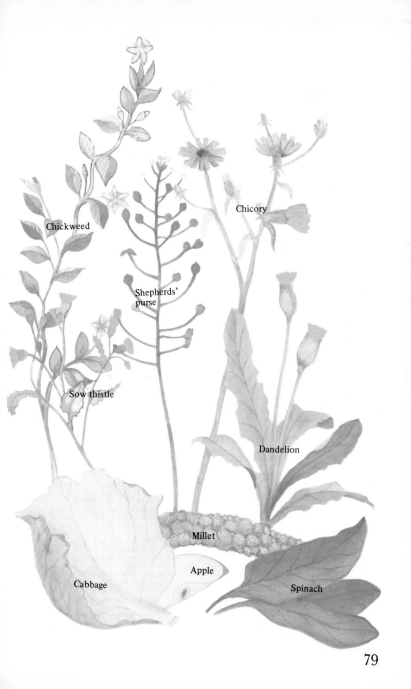

Chickweed

Chicory

Shepherds'
purse

Sow thistle

Dandelion

Millet

Cabbage

Apple

Spinach

79

throughout the year and when unobtainable and also for a change the following can be used – seeding heads of shepherd's purse, young dandelion leaves, young sowthistles, chicory, tender heart of cabbage, Brussels sprouts and slices of sweet apple or pear. During the breeding season Zebra Finches have a habit of taking any small movable items including green food into their nests which can result in sandwich nests being built. To prevent this from happening it is advisable to tie the green into small bunches so they are too heavy for the birds to carry yet can be pecked at with ease. This may cause the breeder a little more trouble but nevertheless it will often save some nests of valuable eggs. Some breeders are not in a position to get a continuous supply of fresh green foods for one reason or another and when not obtainable freshly sprouted seeds offer a valuable stopgap. The sprouting seeds contain the seed germ which is so highly nutritious and easily assimilated by both adult and young birds. Seeds can be sprouted quite simply by first soaking them in clean cold water for some twenty four hours in small shallow dishes and then putting them in a warm place until sprouts of about one eighth of an inch (3 mm) appear. The seeds mostly used for this purpose are the various millets, canary, wheat and oats. If the seeds are prepared at daily or two day intervals the breeder can have a constant supply of valuable green food always on hand.

In addition to giving the birds plenty of good food and clean water they must also be supplied with grits and other mineral containing elements if they are to remain constantly in a healthy state. It is surprising how great a quantity of these materials are eaten by such small birds as Zebra Finches. Grits are needed by the birds for grinding their food into the right consistency so that it can readily be absorbed. The grits constantly grinding against each other and the food in the gizzard causes the cutting edges to wear and become smooth. When the grits become ineffective they are expelled and have to be replaced and this process goes on throughout the birds' life. This being so, it is vitally important that they always have the opportunity of getting replacements whenever necessary. Grits such as crushed limestone, crushed flints and crushed oyster shells are readily obtainable in the right sizes from all good seed stores. These grits can be given separately or mixed together as the owner wishes.

Large quantities of calcium are required by Zebra Finches and the two main sources of this material are cuttlefish bone and dried crushed domestic hens egg shells. The former should be given both in pieces and also in crushed form and again is obtainable from seed stores. Shells from freshly broken hens eggs should be thoroughly dried and then crushed into very small pieces with a rolling pin or similar object. Sea and river sand, roughly powdered chalk and old mortar rubble, are other good sources of grits and mineral elements. Without the supply of grits etc. Zebra Finches cannot develop bones, muscles and feathers needed for the development of strong healthy vigorous birds.

Zebra Finches consume quite considerable quantities of water for birds of their size and their water vessels must always be kept filled especially during warm weather and when young are in the nests. Baths are necessary both in cage and aviary as Zebra Finches frequently take baths to keep their feathers clean and tight.

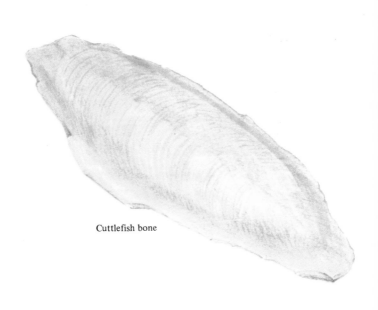

Cuttlefish bone

Chapter 9

Zebra Finches as Exhibition Birds

During the past dozen years or so Zebra Finches have become increasingly popular as exhibition birds and separate sections for them are to be found at most shows up and down the country. This is not really surprising as Zebra Finches have so much to recommend them as exhibition birds in addition to being delightful aviary birds. They are quite easy to train for show work, their show cages are light and compact, and they themselves are excellent travellers. It is now quite usual for fanciers who have kept and bred Zebra Finches for a few seasons to want to exhibit some of the stock they have bred. Breeders always get a thrill when they find the birds bred in their own aviaries are well up amongst the winning pairs.

Much of the advancement in exhibiting Zebra Finches is undoubtedly due to the efforts of The Zebra Finch Society in encouraging Cage Bird Societies to put on good Zebra Finch classifications at their shows and donating special prizes for competition. The Zebra Finch Society also evolved the excellent standard show cage and created a Panel of competent judges of Zebra Finches. This support by The Zebra Finch Society and its Area Societies has put Zebra Finches in a very strong position as exhibition birds.

It will be realised at once that there must be quite a lot in exhibiting other than having good type birds and sending them to shows. When Zebra Finches have been living in an aviary or a large cage and then are suddenly put into a show cage they are naturally somewhat wild and unsteady. Unless a Judge can look carefully at a pair without them being all over the cage a proper appraisal of their merits cannot be made. Many otherwise excellent pairs have failed to get placed in their class through simply being unsteady and therefore not judgeable.

All birds required for showing need a period of show training before they are actually exhibited. The first thing that should be done is to catch up the possible show birds and from them select those which are to be trained. These selected birds should be put into stock cages with the sexes apart and allowed to settle down for two or three weeks. When they have steadied the show pairs can then be matched and one or two pairs put into a cage. The next step is to introduce the birds to the show cages and this can be done by hanging over the open door of the front of their stock cage a mock or old show cage with the door open so that the birds have free access. They can be encouraged to enter the show cage by putting in some fresh green or a millet spray. It is surprising how quickly Zebra Finches will learn to go into a show cage and become quite steady in their smaller surroundings. When the owner feels the pairs are ready each pair can then be shut in a show cage first for a few hours and then for progressively longer periods. Every bird selected will not have the same steady nature and changes may have to be made with some of the pairs that have been previously matched. When the birds are steady in their show cages and ready to go to an exhibition there are certain formalities which have to be made.

The exhibitor should select the shows where the birds are to be entered and write to the secretary well before the show date for a schedule and entry form. Lists of shows are published in 'Cage & Aviary Birds' from time to time and Specialist Societies notify their members of the events receiving their support. The entry form should be filled in as indicated and any special prizes to be competed for should be nominated on the entry form. When completed, this, together with the necessary entry fees, should be sent on to the Show Secretary well before the closing date. In due course before the show the exhibitor will receive the class labels which should be stuck on to the centre of the front rail of the show cages. Great care must be taken to see that the right cage labels are on the cages containing the birds in the class in which they were entered on the entry form. The birds should be taken to the show in good time for judging and if possible the evening before the day of the show as this will give the birds a few hours to settle down. When the birds arrive back from the show they should be returned to their stock cage and given a tit-bit as a reward. Pairs should not be shown too frequently otherwise they will lose their high condition and their breeding potential may be adversely affected. Now to get back to the selection of possible show birds. It is recommended that the Zebra Finch Society show standards are borne well in mind and the colour description of the individual kinds strictly adhered to. Below will be found The Zebra Finch Society show standards.

Show Standards

Condition to be essential. Birds should not receive any award unless in perfect show condition. (Missing, ragged or soiled feathers, and missing claws or toes constitute show faults.)

Type. Bold throughout and of the 'Cobby' type, giving the birds a look of substance; wings evenly carried to root of tail.

Markings (Cocks). Chest bar distinct and clear cut, *not less* than one eighth of an inch wide (3 mm) and of even width throughout. Side flankings should be prominent, extending from wing butts to end of rump and decorated with round, clearly defined white spots. Beak coral red with feet and legs deep pink. All markings where applicable to be clear and hens. Hens as for cocks less cheek patches, chest bar and side flankings; beak a paler shade of red or yellow. Male markings on hens are definite show faults.

Zebra Finches can only be shown in true pairs, i.e., a cock and a hen at Specialist societies Patronage Shows. A pair must always consist of two birds of the same mutation. This means that say a pair of Penguins must be *both* Penguin Normal Greys or *both* Penguin Fawn. A pair of Dilutes must be a pair of Silvers or a pair of Creams. New exhibitors should take special note of this and not mix up breeding pairs with show pairs.

The above covers the main points in exhibiting and the exhibitor will gain a more complete knowledge of this side of the hobby by visiting Open Shows and attending local Members Shows and Club discussions. It is a good idea for Zebra Finch breeders to join their local Cage Bird Society so they are in touch with other Fanciers in their immediate district. Newcomers will find membership a great help in getting to know more about their favourite birds.

Although Zebra Finches can be shown in any kind of suitable show cage they can only complete for the majority of Special prizes if they are shown in Zebra Finch Society Standard show cages. These standard cages can be bought from good bird shops or through advertisements in 'Cage & Aviary Birds' or the exhibitor can make his own or get them made locally. For those who wish to make their own cages the specification of The Zebra Finch Society standard show cage is given below. This specification must be followed in all details –

Specification

Size: Overall measurement 12″ long, 11¼″ high, 6″ wide.

Wood: Top, sides and false roof. Back good quality 4 mm ply.

Door: Round 3½″ diameter centre 5⅜″ from floor of cage 2⅞″ from sides, one wire loop.

Front rail: Height 2⅜″ from floor, turn out feeder door on left hand side of front rail 3½″ long by 1⅜″ deep; sloping cut at edge. 16-gauge escape bar fixed to door. Door fastened by ⅞″ brass desk turn painted black. Zinc clip screwed to inside of door to carry white plastic drinker, ¾″ 16-gauge S-hook on outside.

Perches: Length 4″ overall measured from the back of the cage, ⅜″ diameter with plain boss at back 1″ diameter projecting ⅜″. Perches to be fixed 4⅜″ from floor of cage and 4″ apart on the centre line of the cage horizontally.

Wire front: Comprising 23 wires, 16-gauge mesh, ½″ centre to centre, double punched bar at top set 3/16″ apart, for fixing two wires left at top and bottom.

Top: Width 5¼″, carrying hole 1¼″ diameter, centre 1¾″ from back of cage.

Colour: Inside painted white, outside and wire front black.

Floor covering – any millet or mixture suitable for Zebra Finches.

A Zebra Finch Society standard show cage

Cages will need to be kept clean at all times and exhibitors may find that a little touching up of chipped paint work or periodically completely repainting is needed. Only the best quality non lead containing paint should be used and this be allowed to get thoroughly dry and hard before using to house any birds.

Chapter 10

Health and Sickness

Taken as a species Zebra Finches are healthy hardy little birds that thrive well in many circumstances without any undue fuss on their owner's part. This of course is providing the birds are strong, well housed, and correctly fed. Nevertheless at times a bird may fall sick through some cause or other and this will necessitate some first aid treatment. The most frequent cause of sickness amongst Zebra Finches seems to be colds or chills which if not attended to at once can develop into something much more serious. Colds or chills are mostly contracted during cold, wet or foggy weather when the birds are moulting or get in a draught and of course early bred young birds can be very susceptible.

As soon as a bird is seen sitting about with its feathers all fluffed up and its head tucked under its wing or is heard sneezing it should be caught up at once and caged and taken into a warm even temperature of about 75°F (24°C). It is surprising how quickly a bird will respond and recover when given extra heat; when fully recovered a bird that has been sick should not be returned to its usual aviary too quickly as this could cause a recurrence of the condition. Four drops of syrup of buckthorn will be found very useful in helping a bird to recover, this should be added to the drinking water that has first been boiled. In addition to the bird's usual seed a millet spray should be given but all green food should be withheld. A small quantity of soft food or wholemeal bread moistened with glucose and water will often tempt a sick bird to eat.

It is extremely important that strict hygiene is carried out when dealing with a sick bird and the hands of the owner should be washed in disinfected water both before and after handling a sick bird. If this is not done it is so very easy for harmful germs to be passed on to healthy stock in the same aviary. All cages and utensils that have actually been in contact with a sick bird should be thoroughly disinfected before being used again.

Although I have found that many species of birds are subject to Enteritis I have not yet found this condition amongst Zebra Finches. This is not to say that it does not happen but it must be quite unusual for Zebra Finches to contract this nasty condition. The symptoms are similar to that of a chill accompanied with green stained and sticky droppings. If noticed quickly enough a sick bird may well be saved by taking it into a warm room as with a chill and adding to the drinking water four drops of Sulphamethazine, 16% solution. Four drops of this solution should be added to the water for three days, then two days should be missed, and then given for two further days. Any dirty or fouled feathers should be gently cleaned by washing with a mild disinfectant and warm water. If the Enteritis is not too far advanced the chances of recovery are good but the affected bird will need careful treatment for a few weeks before being returned to its usual aviary or cage. Any bird that has been subjected to extra heat should be gradually hardened off and not suddenly returned to its normal condition. Because of the contagious nature of Enteritis very special care regarding disinfecting must be taken. There are many disinfectants on the market and it is always advisable to have a bottle on hand in the birdroom in case of an emergency.

If allowed to put on surplus weight and thereby losing their hard condition Hen Zebra Finches are liable to become egg bound. Other causes of egg binding are cold wet weather, lack of egg shell building materials in the hens' systems and hens not being fully matured or being bred from inbred stock. The possibility of egg binding occurring can in practically all cases be avoided by breeding during good weather from fully developed adult hens that have had access to plenty of calcium and other necessary minerals. Should a case of egg binding occur the affected bird should be caged and taken into a warm even temperature and six drops of glycerine added to the drinking water. When the bird is caught it is helpful to put a drop of warm olive oil directly on the vent. The main treatment is warmth which allows the contracted muscles to relax and start to work normally. Should a hen become egg bound because of a soft or weak shelled egg the bird is much more difficult to treat because such an egg does not properly respond to the muscular contractions. A good 70% of the hens that have suffered from soft shelled eggs are of little use for further breeding during that season. It takes a considerable length of time for hens to build up the necessary mineral reserves in their systems. This fact points very conclusively to the fault of the owner in not supplying sufficient minerals and grits to the stock all through the year and not just prior and during the breeding season. When a hen has laid the egg she should not be returned immediately to the breeding quarters but should be gradually hardened off and then given a spell of rest in a flight before any attempt is made to re-mate her.

A condition that can affect Zebra Finches and other small Finch-like birds that spend much of their time in cages is foot sores. In

Spraying cage with pesticide or disinfectant.

most instances the sores on the feet of the birds are brought about by small pieces of grit or husks of seed becoming attached to the toes by soft droppings which harden into lumps and later become infected. If these hard lumps are left they will form sores and the birds will most likely lose some of the ends of their toes. Immediately any bird is seen to have something unusual adhering to its feet it should be taken from its quarters and put into a show cage or some similar small cage. The affected foot should be gently bathed with an antiseptic disinfectant and warm water until the hard matter softens and can be crumbled away. No attempt should be made to clean the foot when in a dry state otherwise toes can be permanently damaged. After softening and gently removing the hard matter the foot should be dried with cotton wool and well dusted with a good antiseptic powder. It is important that the perches of the treatment cage are kept perfectly clean by daily washing with disinfectant and warm water. It usually takes about a week or ten days for foot sores to clear up.

A few birds die each year from heart attacks or strokes and for such sudden conditions there is nothing that the breeder can do.

However it is well known that over fat birds are much more liable to heart trouble than those in a fit state, so every possible precaution should be taken to prevent birds from becoming fat through over feeding or through lack of exercise. It is also thought that diseases of the liver are generally due to surplus fat, fortunately Zebra Finches rarely seem to suffer in this direction.

Some Zebra Finches are prone to getting over long toe nails especially when kept in cages for long periods and if they are not trimmed, toes or a leg may get caught up and damaged. Because of their small size special care must be taken when handling Zebra Finches for clipping their nails. The birds should be held gently but firmly in the hand taking a leg between the thumb and first finger leaving the toes exposed. The surplus nail should then be cut away with a small pair of sharp scissors always making sure the cuts are made clear of the central blood vessel. Once nails have been trimmed they usually need doing periodically so their nails need to be examined from time to time.

I think that when the reader has given thought to keeping Zebra Finches he will realise that they are most suitable birds for keeping under many and varied conditions. The cost of keeping Zebra Finches is comparatively small when compared with most other kinds of pet cage and aviary birds.

APPENDIX A.

The efficient and able Secretary of The Zebra Finch Society since 1962 is J. A. W. Prior, 103, Horncastle Road, Lee, SE12 9LF, who would be pleased to give details of the benefits of membership of the Society.

Index